An American

A Tale of Remembering and Forgetting

a hybrid memoir

Anisa Rahim

SPUYTEN DUYVIL
NEW YORK CITY

Thank you to the editors of the journals where the following was first published :

The Newest Americans : Stories from the Global City for *A Photograph* and *On Cows*

Hotel Amerika, Volume 19 Winter 2021 for *Peacock*

Common Ground Review, Fall Winter 2021 for *7 Things I Know About Him*

OJAL : Open Journal of Arts and Letters for *The Train*

Thank you to *[Pank] Magazine* for selecting *American Meo* in the 2019 Book Contest longlist for Nonfiction.

© 2023 Anisa Rahim
ISBN 978-1-959556-37-4

Cover art © Anisa Rahim

Library of Congress Cataloging-in-Publication Data

Names: Rahim, Anisa, author.
Title: An American Meo : a tale of remembering and forgetting: a hybrid
   memoir / Anisa Rahim.
Other titles: Tale of remembering and forgetting: a hybrid memoir
Description: New York City : Spuyten Duyvil, [2023]
Identifiers: LCCN 2023013334 | ISBN 9781959556374 (paperback)
Subjects: LCSH: Rahim, Anisa--Family. | East Indian American
   women--Biography. | East Indian Americans--Biography. | Rahim,
   Anisa--Travel--India. | Meo (Indic people)--History. | Mevāt
   (India)--History.
Classification: LCC E184.E2 R34 2023 | DDC 973/.04914092
   [B]--dc23/eng/20230526
LC record available at https://lccn.loc.gov/2023013334

For My Parents

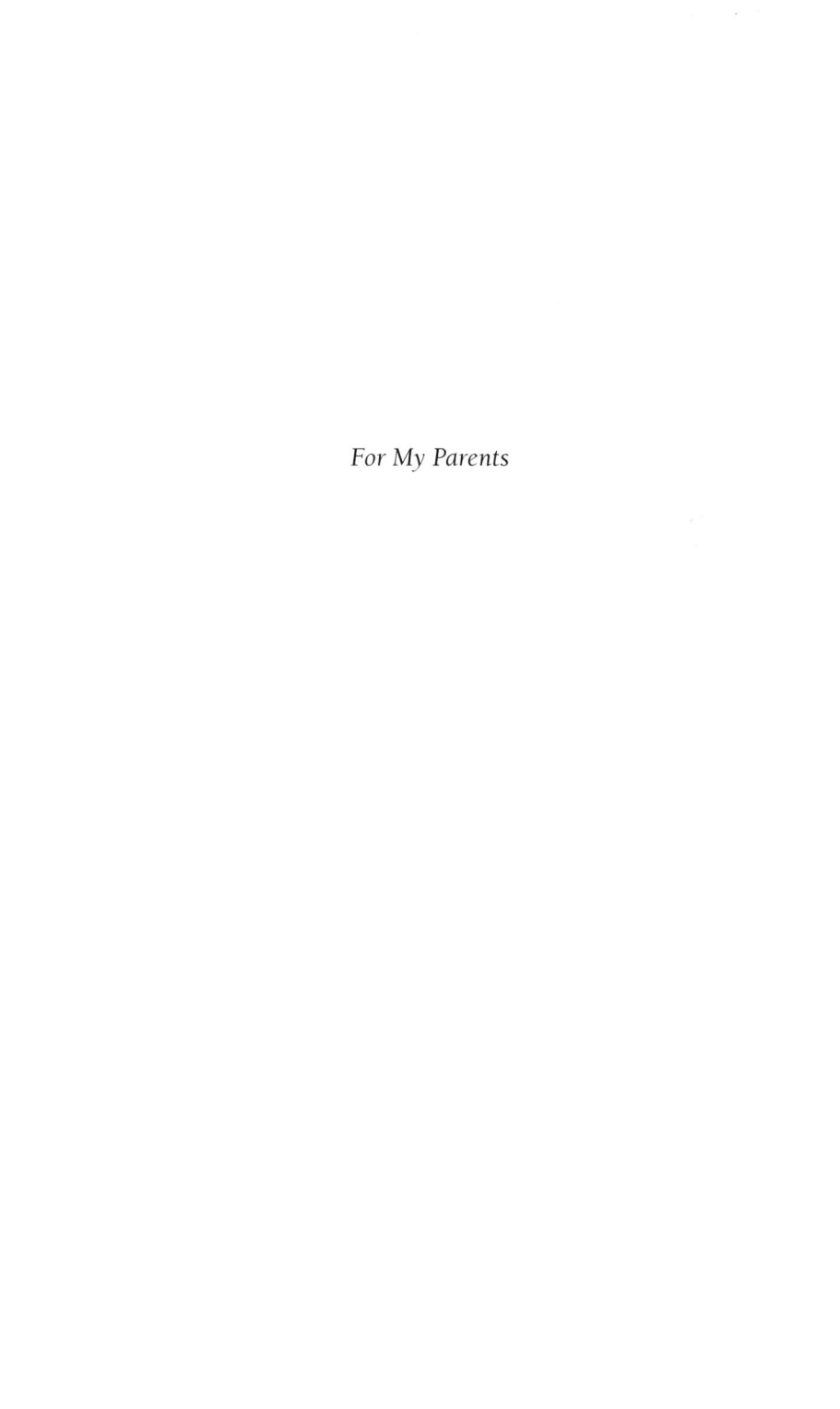

Contents

I.

Family Tree   8
Wali-ji, Friend of God   11
A Photograph   13
Song of a Nightingale   22
On Cows   26

II.

The Kothi   31
Beginnings of a Friendship between a Mosque
    and a Banyan Tree   37
Lands   39
Speak with Hands   42
Stay   45

III.

Hindu or Muslim, Both or Neither   53
Verse   60
Monkey Man   61
Delhi   64

IV.
On Language   67
Glossary of Meo Terms   74
Footsteps   75
A Changing Gurgaon   77
Kahain Loo (Where Are You?)   80
Meo or Minas   82

V.

My Bag is Not Full of Bombs   88
On Kashmir   89
Excerpts from the Srinagar High Court's Decision,
    April 2014   100

VI.

Finding Rimbaud   105
'Amriki'   108
The Silk Route   112
Facing the Tomb of Abdul Rahim Khan   115
Peacock   119
Anarkali: A Story in Five Parts   121

VII.

Jodhpur, Rajasthan   129
An American Meo   131
Close to the Land   139
A Brief Index of Crops   142
Crazy Horse   143
7 Things I Know about Him   147
Radio Mewat   149

VIII.

Inherit   155
I Retell Mirasi Stories   159
The British   164
The National Archives   167
Biography of Yasin Khan   174
A Timeline of Activities   181
Widowed   184

IX.

My Mother Speaks   189
Mom's Recipes   198

X.

The Train   203
Google Alert   206
Good Books   211

I.

Family Tree

Mother's Side
Khuda Baksh
Munni- Yasin Khan m. Rasuli

|

Tayyab- Hamid- Asghar- Akhtari- Surwuri- Asghari- Afsari

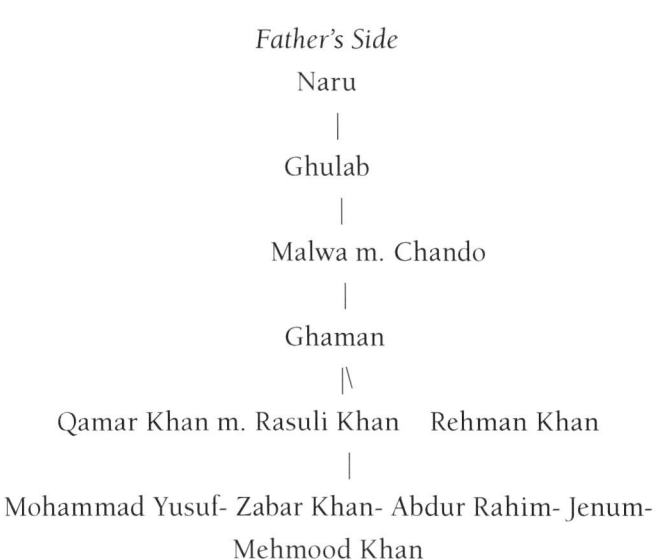

Father's Side
Naru
|
Ghulab
|
Malwa m. Chando
|
Ghaman
|\
Qamar Khan m. Rasuli Khan   Rehman Khan
|
Mohammad Yusuf- Zabar Khan- Abdur Rahim- Jenum-
Mehmood Khan

Wali-ji, Friend of God

I slipped onto a tiger. I stroked and petted its fur. The tiger carried me upwards when my calves began to pierce. They saw me from afar, down below. Their eyes peering upwards, looking curiously.

I could hear their voices. I wanted to lose these voices.

Each word paining me, diving deep into the skin. The calls and echoes empty. Like a thorn, I pull the words out. *Are they really necessary?*

I ride further away from them. I can speak to the bird that dazzles between the trees. The bird and I can look at one another, the speaking of eyes. The dropping of fear. Fear that falls heavy and melts gracefully into the mountain. It makes a river of gravel and dust and fallen, black leaves.

I walk, even in the bitter cold wind. Sometimes, days at a time. Only a shawl wrapped around.

Again, the fear around my ankles.

I can tell from the way that blue hangs with the closing of the sun that change is somewhere nearby. The smell of burnt wood and rabbit droppings. And that is why it is necessary to hold it, with the tiger between my legs.

Dried leaves crunching in my mouth, caught in the gaps of my teeth, but still an easy swallow.

They may not understand these disappearances, the peering eyes below. Confused, not lucid like the eyes of the tiger between my legs. They do not know how these silences, this barrenness, the slow detection of the small, seismic rumblings will feed us all.

We cannot be afraid to lose.

And like this, the days pass, the clothes grow soiled, the hair in small, rough ringlets, finally unruly.

A Photograph

1998. In my third year of college at the University of Chicago, my Urdu professor, C.M. Naim, asks me one day during a class break, "Where are you from?"

Our class is held in his small corner office with a wooden table surrounded on all sides by filled bookshelves. Urdu is a dying language of North India, a blend of Sanskrit, Persian and Arabic. My classmates have scampered for bathroom, smoke and coffee excursions. For months, I struggle in his class, repeatedly and wrongly conjugating Urdu tenses. I invoke his wrath when I despoil the language. Most of us in the class with South Asian heritage, born in the U.S., do not know our mother tongue with fluency.

"My parents were born in Mewat." I reply. "A cluster of villages outside of Delhi that even those in Delhi do not know about. They don't speak 'pure' Urdu but a local dialect."

He raises his eyebrows. C.M. Naim is a leading Urdu scholar in the U.S., if not the world. We are studying Urdu from the textbook he has authored.

"Yes, I know of Mewat. Even I would have trouble understanding that dialect." He says gently. "Interesting. You have a very interesting history. You must read about it."

He compels me towards the Regenstein Library's fifth floor stacks, one of the only collections in the world that brims with so many obscure books on South Asia. That afternoon I am the only person there, lost in rows of metal shelves under dim lights. As I fumble through cloth-bound, hardback texts, an overexposed black and white print photograph in Pratap Aggarwal's *Caste, Religion and Power* stares back at me. In the quiet light of this behemoth library's book stacks, I find a familiar face.

I know this man.

The college librarian, eyes squinting above her reading glasses, interrupts me. She is standing at the far end of the shelves, bellowing, her warning resembling a reprimand: the lights have to be shut off. Now it is just the two of us in the fifth floor book stacks.

A folded white paper with the book's reference code floats like a feather to the ground.

I leave *Caste, Religion and Power,* on the shelf, too much to hold for one day, and venture outside. Snowflakes dissolve into my black coat. Ice crunches beneath the soles of my black boots. How strange and eerie these Chicago winters seemed at first; I did not even own a winter coat before I moved to this city. The wind now howls and cuts past my cheeks. The night is starless, wondrous.

Chaudhry Yasin Khan

In *Caste, Religion, and Power,* I encounter my grandfather's picture. My grandfather is Yasin Khan. He is born in November 1896, at the cusp of a new century in Mewat. Mewat is a geographical area in north India spanning the states of Haryana, Rajasthan and Uttar Pradesh. It is distinct because it is home to the Meos, a Muslim tribal group. The Mirasis, North Indian folk storytellers, say that the Goddess Bedmata inscribes unique lines of destiny on Yasin Khan. He dies long before I am born.

After college, in the years to come, I gather stories about him, but at the time I encounter his photograph in the Regenstein Library, I only vaguely know that he is my grandfather.

Over several years, I learn about his role in the 1930s peasant resistance against the hike in agricultural taxes.

His fight with the Raja of Alwar. His construction of the first high school in Mewat with a sympathetic Britisher. His struggles in the Indian Independence Movement and the ways he tries to stop his people from leaving their land and migrating to Pakistan during Partition. How the Yasin Brayne Meo High School that he helps to construct becomes a home for Partition refugees. The terrible grief at his death that spreads through thousands of people in hundreds of villages, widowing all of Mewat. In the backdrop of current seismic social and economic shifts in Meo villages, I do not know how to make sense of it all, except to gather story after story.

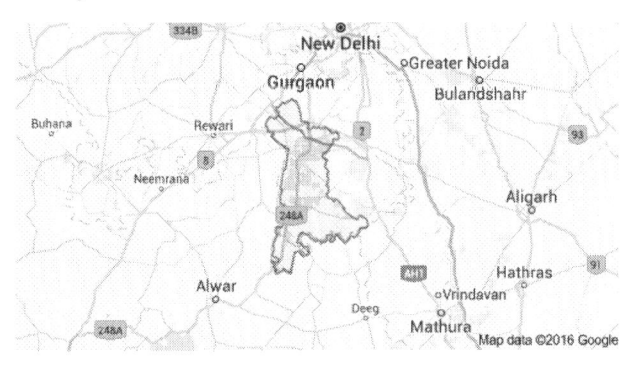

After seeing the photograph, shame crawls over my body. Shame rises from the pores of my skin and remains on the tips of my arm hair. It is a shiver that is not part of winter. I am not sure where the shame stems from, only that my life is incongruous. The flitting around. The socializing, the banter constrained to one level of conversation. When I first move from my hometown in Florida, I hate this cold city and college, wildly homesick, but now I am caught in the mirth of social gatherings. I was never all that indulgent, never that wild, but indulgent enough to feel a guilt that tugs. But guilt based on what, even I do not know.

The guilt of frivolity, I finally realize. I return to the book stacks. Again, a piece of paper floats to the ground.

The guilt of ignorance.

I tell my roommate about the photograph. Her parents, Chicago suburbanites, hail from a remote province in northwest Pakistan.

"He looks Pathan," she says, referring to her own background. Together we stare at my grandfather's picture in meaningful silence. We do not say much more about the photograph or the text.

At the University of Chicago, the checkered black and white floors of the Music building connect the Philosophy and Humanities buildings. During my third year, as I rush from one class to another, I hear a piano playing Chopin. It is a sonata I had also learned to play, soulfully, body leaning into the piano, if never entirely well or completely. As I rush to class, my mind darts through readings in theory. Theories of syncretism, lost histories, postcoloniality, subject and text, observer and observed.

These theories coalesce when just a few weeks later in my South Asian Civilizations class, we watch a documentary about agricultural women laborers in northern India. The women could be from my parent's village; one even resembles my aunt but with a chipped tooth. We visited these villages for harried two-week stays every few years and me, keen to photograph each piece of it even then.

Dung-caked huts and women in *purdah*, their long *dupattas,* practically down to their waist, a long drape of billowing cloth. The men, in turbans, crouching, smoking *bidis*. At sixteen, I knew that these images all had to be captured, viewed again in the red light of a darkroom on a print that floated in a developing tray. Prints collected in shoeboxes, negatives with frayed edges accumulating.

Women in the Village

Now as a college student, I do not know whom to tell about this confrontation with the past. If I can even admit my simultaneous elation and shame. Others I meet hardly have any relatives back in India or if they do, they live in posh residential urban areas, still partial mirrors for their diasporic counterparts. In contrast, many of my relatives reside in villages. Or should I proudly proclaim, *I come from a lineage of the oppressed, the enslaved, the rebellious...what I really mean to say is the broken-hearted.*

In the auditorium where my South Asian Civilizations class is held, the women on the screen are subjects wrapped in a cellophane of patriarchy, liberalization, and resistance.

I do not know what all this means only that something thumps beneath my blue and white blouse. My father always wanted me to study at Oxford; for Indians, the sign of a true elite education. I had after all grown up playing Chopin, experiencing such intimacy as if the music had been crafted and recorded for me. Now, in class, the very nearest to me are being excavated, displayed, discussed so as not to be forgotten. *Only were they ever known?*

I can see the piano music: stray sheets of five-bar lines filled with dancing black circles coupled with stems, some of the stems possessing leaves, being wildly strewn across the checkered black and white floors. A different music and language is leading me elsewhere. I feel myself leaving one world and set of concerns to enter deeply into another.

Soon after, I return to my parents' home in Florida. I confront my mother in the kitchen. We are always in the kitchen. My mother is in a long, flowery nightgown holding a ladle in her hand. She stirs a pot as she gazes at the television screen, usually an Indian soap opera she watches with fixed intensity. Her mouth is slightly open in alarm at the events unfolding on the celluloid.

"I never knew him. You never told me who he was," I insist. I pace between the dining room and the kitchen. I pick up a napkin which I dangle and pretend to clean surfaces.

"That is not true. How else would you recognize him?"

I want to say that I thought you were illiterate, unknowing. I even thought you were a fool. My brothers and I called her a simpleton with her stories about the village, as if the village could be anything more than a place without electricity and roads. I never believed her stories could rise from the page.

"Flies in the head," my mother continues. "*Dhora pad gaya!* This daughter of mine. When will you be subdued?"

A fly finds its way near my left earlobe. It whirs like an airplane. Will it bite or just whisper? The fly grows louder than my mother's dismissiveness. The fly tries to venture down an ear shaft, then circles my head. I wave my hand in irritation and blink.

"I have to nap now." She stirs the pot one last time and puts the wooden spoon down on a green plastic plate on the counter. "Wake me up with tea."

My mother naps each afternoon. Sometimes, during these afternoon slumbers in a room of pastel green curtains, she dreams. Dreams that reveal. As when a cousin had run away from home, escaping onto a train, disappearing into a crowd. No one told my mother that had in fact happened. When she pressed the matter with a relative, months later, the story spilled forth like a broken necklace. Words like beads slid and bounced on a wooden floor across the room, accompanied by my mother's requisite gasps.

I crave such dreams, her gift of knowing. Instead, I fall into a black wash of sleep each night, waking each morning, unsure where all the hours have gone.

Over the next two years, I read and read and read. Books, texts, and words give me meaning that led me deeply elsewhere, like a plunge below the ocean that shows other life-forms below the hinting blue of the surface. One afternoon, as I become preoccupied with Mewat, asking my mother questions for which she does not have answers, my mother dreams of my grandfather. My mother refers to him as *Bhaiyya* meaning 'brother' which of course he was not but she and her siblings heard everyone else refer to him as such and that became his designation for years to come. I wake her up with a mug of tea inscribed with "World's Greatest Mother" in a background of red cartoonish brick carefully placing it on the nightstand near the table lamp.

"I dreamt of him," she mumbles. "He was in the room. He patted me on the head and began to speak to me." She stops. "Only now I cannot remember what he said."

I frown. "You do not want to remember. Your longing will rise to the surface and you too will have flies in your head."

In Florida, in the back of our house, there is a dock that overlooks the canal that leads a few meters away into the ocean. The ocean shines. Sometimes, it frowns. Rocks, waves, dips, hurtles. It is easy to watch the ocean and realize that both certainty and uncertainty exist side by side. The certainty that the ocean will be there. The uncertainty of its form, its mood. I grow up mirroring the ocean in my mutability, like the stages of a moon that is quarter, half, full. I wait for those nights, partially unexpected, on evening walks through the neighborhood when the moon shines on the ocean, the light shimmering silver on the black water, against a restless wind.

Song of a Nightingale

When we are in primary school, the bus drops my brother, Arshad, and I near the Community Centre, a mile and half from our house in Florida. Once or twice, my mother oversleeps or gets so wrapped up in her cooking that she forgets the time and that we are waiting. I sullenly sit on the curb as elderly men and women go inside for the early bird bingo game. Arshad, thin and lanky then, kicks gravel in the parking lot. "Looks like mom forgot. She'll realize soon."

Soon enough her Buick pulls into the parking lot, making a swift turn. Both of us sigh in relief. In those moments of waiting, fear of how we get home- with whom- what if an evil stranger came by- flashes through our minds. Fears of hunger begin too. What if we are stranded here? Would we starve? Often mom brings snacks for us, despite it only being a short car ride, usually cookies and a fruit drink in a square cardboard box. In one such incident, Arshad decides that we should walk home.

"Walk home?"

"We can do it. Let's go." We put on our backpacks and walk on the street lined with homes, a steady but unthreatening stream of cars passing by. We meet mom along the way near the golf course.

For that lapse, we have leverage on her for days to come. She allows it initially but soon learns that we are milking the incident for far too much.

"Who told you to walk? You don't know how to use the pay phone in the Community Center?"

Arshad realizes she has a point and becomes silent. We never want to concede she has a point.

But one day when mom arrives, she is stone silent. Her eyes brim with tears.

"Your grandmother died. They called me." She does not say anything more. Arshad and I are stunned. Her silent grief is too much for us.

When we reach home, we watch her tears fall into the teapot over the stove. She has deep brown circles under her fright-filled eyes. Arshad, five years older than me, puts his arms around her. He pats the back of her head.

I hardly remember my grandmother's face, though I am urged to greet her often that one long summer when I am five years old that we spend in the *kothi,* the family home that my grandfather had begun to construct before Partition. Then the electricity went out for hours at a time. Women would gather around us, their fans flapping, coming close then squaring away. A short burst of cold wind, then the air hanging heavily. I envy the grace with which their hands circled.

Years later I take a fan back with me to Florida and try to replicate the circling wrist motion, even though the central air conditioning does not require these gusts of cooling air. That summer I might have run towards my grandmother but admittedly, I now only recall an old woman with missing teeth who slightly frightens me. How the woman beckons me with her arms, *come here,* and how I, a mere five years old, forever wearing anklets, flee in the opposite direction giving the excuse that I have to rush away to play.

Months after my grandmother's death, I remember my mother's grief on that afternoon school ride. I am sitting in her Buick that she has covered with midnight blue terry cloth covers that have accumulated cookie and chip crumbs. We are driving back from the mall. Our outings consist of wandering through a department store in search of her infamous 'pant-shirt' outfits, a black pant and a collared patterned shirt. In all her thirty plus years as an immigrant, my mother never wore a skirt or even jeans for that matter.

Our outing includes a stop at Burger King on Highway 19 in our sleepy small retirement town. Today, we did not find her a pant-shirt. Instead, she buys me a new pair of jeans. My mother has a habit of patting me on the backside in public places and I squeal for her to stop embarrassing me and she just replies no, no, you are my daughter. This is her love, without borders or rationale or self-control. Over the years, I learn that the form of her love would never change. Her children would always be children, nestled close to her breast, for the best days of her life were when we were young, mirroring when she was young and close to her mother.

In the backseat of the Buick, I marvel at my jeans and protect the two gallons of milk we had picked up from the grocery store. An old Hindi film song streams from the cassette player. The sweet aching nostalgia of Lata Mangeshkar, dubbed India's nightingale, and Mohammed Rafi.

The song fills me with my mother's sadness and suddenly, inexplicably in the backseat of her car, I cannot stop wiping away the tears, the sobs too muffled even for her to hear. The nightingale tugs and rips away at something in that afternoon sun. She never sees those tears and I never tell anyone else about that afternoon.

On Cows

I would have been a cow, my mother answers
do cows speak and think of one another, of us,

they must
but they move only when slapped by the palm of a hand

derisive click of the tongue, *'huth,'*
when the street throbs with Maruti cars,

scooters, dry air
it is as if they are all alone,

in a field, eating grass,
they might as well be staring at the sky,

the moon hanging from its lip
you can't understand,

and she tells me some days later
about the cow she was gifted once,

such big, pretty eyes
her own eyes grow larger as she says this,

she comes into my bedroom years later
to ask if both her eyes are the same shape

yes, of course, leave me alone,
you are so strange

No, one is slightly larger than the other
ten years later, I would look in the mirror

and realize the same thing about my own eyes
God denied us symmetry at birth

but no, it is the beauty of jagged shapes

II.

The Kothi

2000. An airplane descends. I delight in the thrill of the wheels as they skid against the ground. Stewardesses in red saris smile in relief.

"Do you remember that time that we were forced to land?" I ask my mother seated next to me. This is my first trip to India in six years. The last time it was just the two of us on a trip to India, I was five and our plane made an emergency landing in Pakistan.

"Yes," she says, applying lipstick after a fourteen plus hour flight in anticipation of seeing her relatives. "You were asleep and did not want to get off the plane. There was trouble with the motor. The stewardess carried you down the aisle and pushed you down a slide."

"She left my shoes," I remember.

"I bought you a pair the next day from the local market. And when we did land in Delhi, you said that you wanted to go back to the U.S." She laughs. "Your uncle told you that it is too late to reverse the plane!"

Now that is hardly the case. I am bursting with excitement.

Newly graduated from college, this is my first stay in India as an adult. My disclosed reason for this sojourn is a human rights fellowship. During the last year of college, I organize an activist group, holding teach-ins and engaging in elaborate email debates over politics in South Asia and its Diaspora. Our collective is passionate on everything from religion, language, nation-state boundaries to Hindi cinema. The collective continues but those of us who graduate scatter to other cities. I apply to law school, a curious amalgamation of wanting to do good in the world and not knowing what else to do. I have six months before it begins. I feel endless possibilities for the future as ideas lay claim across two continents. My undisclosed reason, a motivation I cannot verbalize, is that when I close my eyes tightly, I see a map of India in all red. When I open my eyes, I must follow this red.

The airport is empty because it is the middle of the night, the terrific silence of four a.m. anywhere in the world when only the defiant, the troubled, the ones in transit waiting to land on the next patch of soil are awake. My mother waits for her nephew to squeeze his way into Customs to find us, in defiance of proper rules, an exercise of political clout that she unabashedly enjoys. Those are the days that the lines to pass Customs can easily be over an hour or two and our relatives arrive at the airport at the very time the plane is scheduled to land. My cousin greets us with garlands of two-toned marigolds.

Cousins, nephews, her brother buzz around us, grab suitcases and handbags. They stuff them with startling quickness and efficiency into the back of jeeps. Other cousins gift my mother a bouquet of roses which she hands to me; I have never held such a large bouquet.

Cars honk mercilessly, pushing their way through a cacophony of traffic. We reach the *kothi*. The alley is so narrow that the car struggles. Stray cows, cars and rickshaws coalesce near the lemonade stand in the single alley that leads to the *kothi*. The driver slaps a cow on the backside, '*huth*', and honks furiously for rickshaws to clear the path.

The *kothi* has five levels, but the family only resides on the fourth. The remaining three levels include shops, a sweets store, a tailoring shop, fabric and clothing and shoe stores. The fifth level is the roof that overlooks the city of Gurgaon which was a village when my mother grew up there. *Gur* means sugar and *gaon* means the village itself. Now Gurgaon is a city. The *kothi* is in the old part of the city, congested, confused and bursting with disorderly life. Each visit the *kothi* itself transforms only slightly. It has the calming reassurance of a house that everyone in this sprawling family can visit and be assured they will be given tea and fed a meal.

The Kothi

Staircase *Kitchen Window*

From the rooftop, just a few hundred feet away, I can see the mosque that Yasin Khan and the Meos built in the night. For Yasin Khan so many surreptitious activities took place in near darkness; the mosque was a contentious piece of architecture in colonial India as Hindu-Muslim conflicts heightened. I spend hours going up and down those stairs, a hypnotic ascent. I stare from the balcony onto the market below, pacing the roof and surveying the multi-level stores and residences of old Gurgaon.

In the *kothi*, gender norms can be ambiguous. Sometimes, a space, such as the living room, feels as if it's marked for the men. Women are either invited to sit on the couch or only enter to serve food; other times, even a bedroom can have disparate family members seated together on a single bed engaged in a family argument. It is best to stand on the balcony, to seek respite from the flow of human traffic. The sky dims and yet the vegetable market below throbs, ebbs.

One evening, my aunt, whose foot has been injured for some days from a fall, limps up beside me and balances against the railing. When her head is not covered with a shawl, as it is now, she wears her hair in a single, silver tight braid. She hardly speaks to me but today she does so in clipped sentences. Or are they lines of a poem? "This house was once torn down then rebuilt. The mosque was once painted green before it was pink. The streets were once empty before they became full and the entire public came here to buy their vegetables and fruits."

I nod. In this place of unlikely alliances, could not the banyan tree, symbolic of Indian civilization, and the mosque, a newcomer of the 12th century and finding particular expression in 1945 through Yasin Khan, have spoken to one another?

*Beginnings of a Friendship
Between a Mosque and a Banyan Tree*

Outside the *kothi,* a banyan tree with hundreds of coiling tea-colored branches sits in the center of a small park facing a pink mosque.

"I am about 1,000 years old," the banyan tree estimates for the mosque.

"I am twenty days old," the mosque replies. The mosque can barely stretch a finger. There is a large rectangular pool in the middle of the mosque's body. At night, the moon reflects off this water and dances against the sky. People sit beside this pool and admire its reflection.

"Yasin Khan gave you birth," the banyan tree says. "I saw it all before my eyes." There is a short wind and the leaves in its branches shake.

"Allah gave me birth," the mosque replies.

"Regardless, you are beautiful." The banyan tree is not

interested in polemics. *But will you last?* the banyan tree wonders then sighs. *Will any of us last for very long?*

"I am cement and paint. Can these things make you beautiful?"

"I've seen it all. So much comes. Each new wrinkle gives birth to another finger, another palm, a few more wrinkles."

"But that is why you are magnificent," the mosque finally admits.

"I age and grow more and more plentiful. More and more fingers each year. Not like people…"

"I do not know how long I will live," the mosque says.

"You needn't worry. Even if you break, crumble, and fall to pieces, you lived once in mint green and pink with a body of water in your center. For now, you have me as company."

Together we can talk about births, deaths. Growth, stillness. Sadness, foolishness. Rage and those small slivers of ecstasy that rise up from time to time. That live before they are washed away with the rain.

Lands

my
mother
was
my first country.
the first place I ever lived.
　—lands
from "salt" by nayirrah waheed

My mother stays awake late into the night. A circle of women gather under fluorescent lighting. We stay in my niece's bedroom where Bollywood posters adorn every turquoise wall and movie stars stare at us with full, unblinking eyes. My mother's arrival is an excuse for relatives once, twice, thrice removed to convene at the *kothi* and murmur for hours. Long held disputes are mulled over and new ones made. Relatives come in and out of rooms, stage protests, and develop side conversations and alliances in the hallways over shaky marriages, marital prospects, and land disputes. A female cousin, accused of being too sensitive, disappears to the roof, insulted. The women cajole her to come back downstairs. The gossip and the family dramas are endless, tiring, fascinating. A select few remain, stretched out in cots near the kitchen. An even smaller number circle around my mother's bed well past the clock striking midnight.

"I've heard that people," an aged woman wearing

crooked blue glasses begins, "don't die in America."

"People die in America," my mother insists. My mother has left behind flowery Florida nightgowns and pant-shirts for an array of shalwar kamizes and a loosely draped thin scarf on her head at all times. She is radiant, an orb of white light pushing through her complexion. I admire her sudden transformation. When I was little, I was known to stare in wonder at the cluster of stones that sparkled on her rings, her swathe of thick red lipstick. My mother speaks fluently in Mewati, as if she never left.

"Then *bahan-sister*," the woman continues, "what are you doing there? If you have to die, just like the rest of us, then you might as well die amongst us!"

The room laughs, even me, lying on my side in bed, frowning at the cupboard, wanting to sleep at this late hour. We laugh at the truth, and the innocence, and the ignorance of this statement. For some, such as this woman, there could never be a reason to uproot, except the promise of immortality.

Woman in the Village

Rukhsana and Her Son

Speak with Hands

While we stay in Gurgaon, we travel to the interior of Mewat, a drive down a single, solid path, Sohna Road, with overhanging eucalyptus trees that cut into dirt paths. Sohna Road is the tree trunk and the dirt roads are its branches. The car is filled with more passengers than seats, some tilting forward, others squeezed into a corner, a child on a lap- no one bothers with seatbelts- and the window view, beckoning to open fields, the most coveted spot.

On this road trip, we visit one house after another. The residences vary in structure, but nearly all have an open-air courtyard in the middle. The oldest home is made of mud, *kaccha,* naturally cool in summer and warm in winter. The newest one constructed of cement, *pukka,* with multi-colored geometric Indian tiles and extra bedrooms upstairs. All have animals in the vicinity, cows, buffalo and wandering roosters.

Sometimes, there is a phone call to plan these visits. Since my parents are there, then surely a chicken has to be slaughtered; a feast planned. But often, the visits are impromptu. Somehow, a conversation in open-air courtyards from a few years back is easily resumed. Time bears weight and thickness in the village.

Khairat/Feast

Despite numerous visits, the scenes are always a bit unfamiliar, awakening, as if I am seeing these places new with the same curiosity. Meo women, my cousins, walk with a gait. Their hips sway even as their words bite. Mewat may lag behind in female education, deeply embedded in a patriarchal society and lacking the necessary infrastructure, and yet the women are vocal and expressive, hearts laid on their sleeves, as they coo and yell, metaphors wrapped inside their language. *You are as dumb as the brother of wheat, naaj ka bhai.* No filter. Strange men and women pat my head gently with rough, weathered hands. Over the years, I learn some names.

When my relatives say hello, *salaam,* it is said like this: the younger person walks towards the elder person, bows the head slightly and waits for the elder relative to run a hand over the head. Sometimes, relatives will cup the cheek or run hands over your eyes, as if they have been waiting all this time to see your face. When two peers meet, as when I greet my female cousins, we say hello by grabbing hands, more than a handshake, less than an embrace. We speak with hands, a hello where you smell the other person, long remember the texture of skin after their hand has left yours.

Hands- I

Hands- II

Stay

"How long is she planning to stay?" my uncle, Tayyab Hussain, Mamu Tayyab to me, a heavyset man whose eyes shine, asks during this first trip after college.

When Mamu Tayyab enters a room, he expects to be noticed. He anticipates movement, people scurrying away or hurrying towards him in greeting and supplication. When he smiles, we smile with him. When he yells or barks, we are as muted as wooden objects.

Mamu Tayyab is known to do what is right; to have another's back. After Yasin Khan's death, Mamu Tayyab, the eldest of the sons, is designated the leader of the Meos. He is crowned with the turban and marked as chieftain at the *pagdhi bandhana* ceremony. He is gifted land, jewelry, flowers, gold and even an elephant. The Mirasis construct this quatrain about the ceremony:

So many people were invited
the children of Ram and Krishna
Even if you gathered all the people from China
It would still not be equivalent.

In the television game show, *Kaun Banega Crorepati,* the host Bollywood actor Shah Rukh Khan, asks the contestant which politician in India has been elected out of three different states. The answer: Tayyab Hussain.

Mamu Tayyab is charmed that I am here. Yet his eyes also plainly say, *the daughters of this house do not roam.*

He does not receive an answer to his question, interrupted that morning by more pressing matters as he finishes breakfast. During dinner that evening at the dining room table, a formality reserved for politicians and us Americans, my mother responds, "She wants to stay for six months. Don't you?" She is prodding his disapproval that I may decide to forego the fellowship altogether; she does not want me far from home. "She is a flying kite."

"Why? What will she do here?" Mamu Tayyab states. "She should go around with you, do her shopping and then return. What will she do working at an NGO?"

Desire to work in Mewat, like a punctured balloon, shrivels. While many non-governmental organizations registered in Mewat are shells for corruption and misuse of funds, all possibilities are not exhausted. Still before Mamu Tayyab, it is difficult to disagree openly; silent refusal to leave India is the best I can do.

He is the uncle, after all, who houses us each time we visit, ensuring no want is left unattended. As a child, when Mamu Tayyab learns my penchant for Cassata green, yellow and pink ice cream from the downstairs store, I am fed that ice cream every afternoon for two weeks. Another time I complain about the lack of ventilation in the bathroom, leading to a build-up of sweat in summer months; in the midst of other responsibilities, he orders electricians to install a bathroom-ceiling fan the next day.

Tight-lipped, Mamu Tayyab pulls his chair back, stands

up, surveying the dinner table with bowls of uneaten food and dirty plates. He does not say anything further.

In the weeks ahead, I stay icily quiet in front of him. My eyes deny contact, diverging in other directions, a family member's face, wooden furniture pieces, the long tongue and tail of a lizard with star-shaped claws in the corner.

He too refuses to address me.

I make plans to work at an NGO in Delhi during this six month stay.

A white sheet of silence dangles lazily in the wind between us.

Before his death, seven years later, we reconcile twice. During law school, I return for another year on a fellowship and then again for a visit. Each time I shuttle between Delhi and Mewat, geographically close and yet so very different. It is as if Mewat represents the earth, my roots and Delhi, the sky and possibility.

Once, we speak about Shail Mayaram, the anthropologist in Delhi who interviews him and writes a book about Meos, *Resisting Regimes: Myth, Memory and the Shaping of a Muslim Identity,* a treatise for me to study. Shail spends a semester at University of Chicago and how C.M. Naim knows to send me to the bookstacks, but I only meet her in Delhi.

Mamu Tayyab, whose attention is in demand at all times, makes a point to visit a bookstore and buy Shail's book. He offers it to me in a brown paper bag.

The significance of this gesture is not lost on me. When I am at the *kothi,* relatives reprimand me when I try to read;

to be with others is to converse with them, even if it means sometimes sitting reservedly and awkwardly together, crossing our legs and checking our phones to fill gaps of silence because information is passed orally, through sound and gesture.

"She has written a lot," he says. He is proud of himself for finding a gift that conveys recognition. "She has done a lot of research."

I am surprised by his effort.

He softens when he sees me but I forever feel his annoyance at my presence.

I thank him.

The second reconciliation is on the night of Yasin Khan's *Urs*, the Sufi ceremony marking his death. An *Urs* is celebrated with recited couplets and song because it marks not only death but also the wedding of that individual with God. That night, a massive tent is erected on the grounds of the Yasin Brayne Meo High School. Relatives gather under patches of bright light that dot the school grounds. Beyond those lights lies a pool of darkness filled with the distant buzz of mosquitos and the chirping of crickets.

Earlier that week, Mamu Tayyab and I erupt into as close an argument as we would ever have at the dinner table; a cousin shoots me a look of warning and kicks me under my chair for speaking too much mind.

"Is it not time to settle down?" he insists. This question, a prelude to a conversation that he desires, is not part of any existing talk about the day's coming and goings.

Twenty-seven at the time, I do not feel young but nor do I want to settle down. Settling down means not coming to India for such long periods or working with NGO's in Delhi or living separately from my relatives when I am here on long stints.

For years, my relatives do not know what to make of each arrival in India. They bestow me with dozens of new shalwar kamizes, compelling me to abandon my college black goth attire for pastel pinks and purples. They insult local tailors for failing to sew clothes on time. It's a love that overwhelms me. When relatives ask over and over again, "*Man lag raha hain?*" which means, "Is your heart here?" and more generally, "Are you at home here?" I can only nod yes, say yes with shining eyes.

I do not answer Mamu Tayyab.

In the months of what evolves into years of ongoing travel, he must concede that I am fine, without scars or overt signs of damage. Or rather, the scars that come through travails of living in a place simultaneously familiar and foreign are ones of my own choosing. If Yasin Khan travelled with a cloud of protection over him, I wonder if I do not benefit from the shade of that same cloud.

When he presses the question, after years of biting my tongue, I spill forth an unexpected monologue, "I am doing nothing wrong. My perceived shortcomings are my strengths and virtues. I am not doing drugs, I am not stealing, I am interested in social work and human rights- "

I do not speak for very long but it is enough to invite a kick under the table, sharp looks all around.

Mamu Tayyab stands up. Again, he surveys the table of half-eaten dinner plates and soiled napkins as he pulls back his chair. He leaves without saying anything more.

My relatives cluster around me. As much as I tried to come and go to the *kothi* making as little demands as possible, I am now part and parcel of the family dramas that I used to watch ensue around me. I sob for wanting to be in India at all.

My cousin who kicked me concedes, "You are right in his own way. He is right in his own way. What are we to do?"

At the *Urs* ceremony, I am determined not to speak to him for this constructive eviction. Only when Mamu Tayyab stands across me, outside of the Yasin Brayne Meo High School, he puts his arms around my waist and pulls me close to his large protruding belly. We've never actually embraced; I've only ever felt his hand grace my head.

Pained by my silence, he acquiesces to my obstinacy and whispers, "*Aathe rehna*. Keep coming."

My anger, a hot rod, fizzles for the moment.

Stay.

III.

Hindu or Muslim, Both or Neither

> "Your history gets in the way of my memory…
> My memory keeps getting in the way of your history."
> —from "Farewell" by Agha Shahid Ali
>   in *The Country Without a Post Office*

Once, as a child, after a twenty-plus hour flight from Florida, I arrive in Gurgaon and that morning, my mother and I make a trip to the small village of Saint Avardi to pay respects at the grave site of a shrine. We enter the room during a moment of ecstatic song. My mother and I are seated close to the grave, a few meters away from the musicians, cross-legged on the floor, singing *qawwalis* with accordions in hand.

Years later, I learn that we went to the grave of Wali-ji. The literal meaning of Wali-ji is Friend of God, but refers to my great grand uncle, an actual human being who raises Yasin Khan after his own father abruptly drowns chasing his buffalo into a pond. For his spiritual powers, including long meditative wanderings in the Aravalli Mountains, Wali-ji is deemed a saint. His shrine lies in a largely desolate village with only occasional visitors.

Interior of Wali-ji's grave   *Exterior*

Once, as a college student, I wash the living room silver with my mother in the kitchen. It is a Sunday morning ritual where we polish each piece of silverware so that it evolves from a smudged black to gleaming silver. We ignore the Florida sun beyond the sliding doors, a light so bright it imposes a glare, and the swaying palm trees outside, to stay amidst air-conditioning and cool shadows. She and my father argue about their castes, Daimroth and Dhaingal.

"Dhaingals are superior," my mother insists.

My father shakes his head at this claim of superiority, as if it even matters.

Only how can we have a caste when we are Muslim, I wonder.

Then, I learn that Meos have a background both of Islamic Sufism, hence the visit to the shrine, and indigenous Hinduism, hence Meos' caste. My father's caste claims to be descendants of the avatar-God Krishna. The great epic battle of the *Mahabharata* is after all, fought partially in Gurgaon itself. My mother's caste, Dhaingals, claim to be descendants of the god-avatar Rama.

"Do you know," I say to them, as faucet water spurts onto a silver teacup during another round of Sunday morning silver washing, "that your allegiance to caste is derived from Hinduism."

"It is possible," they answer, flinching. I can tell they do not like my conflation of their castes with Hinduism. We are solid Muslims now.

Next, I learn that some relatives don't subscribe to Islamic Sufism and will not visit the grave of Wali-ji. One side of the family deems this a forbidden practice. By now, there are strains of conservative Islamic movements that find music and mixed theologies a desecration of faith. I am horrified at this denial of song.

The British confused it all. They could not grasp a community that was indigenous Hindu but that in the thirteenth century slowly converted to Islam through a Sufi saint, Moinuddin Chishti, who preached, *love for all*. Meos swallowed pieces of this new religion like an unknown fruit.

Leaders decided that India would be a Hindu state and Pakistan would be a Muslim state because in this new nation of clear divisions, one had to make a decisive choice about faith. Yasin Khan however, urged Meos to stay in India so that they would not lose their land and Meos officially declared themselves Muslims.

Today, Meos are still Muslims, though once Hindu-Muslim tribal-agricultural. Today, Meos are a minority of the Indian state, falling into the category of Other Backward Classes, a collective term used by the Government of India for socially and educationally disadvantaged sectors of the population.

Today, I decide that I am a descendant of divinity. Literally, because Wali-ji is a follower of the Sufi Chistiyya order. Spiritually, because Krishna and Rama probably did pass through Mewat and spawn a bloodline. A skeptical scholar, a close friend actually, says this claim to the Hindu gods is an example of an oppressed group laying claim to a history to rehabilitate the cultural self; I decide that he is merely jealous of my origins.

2001. I meet Shail Mayaram, the author of *Resisting Regimes,* the book Mamu Tayyab had gifted me, for the first time at a small lecture-workshop. The workshop is being held by Ramachandra, "Ramu" Gandhi, the grandson of Mahatma Gandhi, at the Habitat Center in New Delhi. During the tea break, I am sitting on the steps outside, a perfect Delhi afternoon where the lawns are lush green and a range of orange-pink flowers bloom. Next to me is a female professor who teaches at the University of Florida. We converse. The irony, I think, of meeting another Indian Floridian in Delhi. Only another woman, Shail herself, crouches down next to me, her sari creating a pool of silk fabric around her feet, and introduces herself. This gesture of kneeling endears me to her for years to come.

"I have read your book," I blurt out. There is so much material in it, her words dense and colliding into one another. I only have vague intimations of where it will lead me. I explain who I am.

She raises her eyebrows. "I am glad people are still reading my book and it is relevant." Then she says to the University of Florida professor, "She is a descendant of the Chistiyya lineage."

For Shail, I am a cultural artifact in the flesh. I can feel the largeness of my own symbolism. The air is electric and the landscape charged with color.

Shail is the scholar whose work will teach me how to read Mewat.

Over the years, Ramu Gandhi gives lectures on religion and philosophy to a small group of no more than ten which I attend from time to time. Ramu Gandhi is taller than his grandfather but has the same unassuming yet alive demeanor. He dresses in a traditional handloom kurta-pajama.

I am daunted but moved by the scholarly discourse in the room. When I do attend, I am the only Muslim present. Ramu Gandhi is aware that I am there. I assume that he is unphased by my presence.

Post-Partition politics in India has rippling effects as various right-wing factions arise to represent both Hindus and Muslims. There are increasing incidents of Islamophobia in India as Muslims are associated with terrorism and social and economic backwardness. Right-wing Hindu groups, like the Bharatiya Janata Party (BJP) and particularly its faction the Rastriya Swayamsevak Sangh (RSS), suspect the loyalty of Indian Muslims to the nation and imply, at times bellow, that they should go to Pakistan and join their brethren.

One afternoon, Ramu Gandhi addresses me, "Did Islam not find its singing voice in South Asia?"

Yes, I think, *yes.*

What I do not know at that moment is that Ramu Gandhi's grandfather, Mahatma Gandhi, knows Yasin Khan. Gandhi comes to Mewat and urges Meos not to leave India during Partition because Meos are "the *rirrh*-the spine of this nation."

Ramu Gandhi continues to lecture on the Indian epic, *The Ramayana,* the quest of the god Rama to rescue his wife Sita from the demon Ravana. Ramu Gandhi wonders about the goddess Sita's exile to the forest after Ram suspects her of infidelity when Ravana abducts her. Was it not wrong for Ram to suspect her chastity, her fidelity? He should not have made her walk through the fire to prove her purity.

Yes, yes.

But is not Sita during her exile dancing in the forest?

I pause. I have never heard this interpretation from Indian feminists. *Maybe.*

Even in the face of exile, he continues, in the face of a wrong, she is not only anguished. She is also a maker of music.

Does Islam not find its singing voice in India? Ramu Gandhi does not repeat this phrase but I do to myself. The Mirasis, the musicians at *Wali-ji's* shrine, the poetry of the mosque are all a piece, a sliver of this voice. They all *belong*.

Yes, yes, yes, yes.
and
yes, yes, yes
and
yes.

Verse

A *Kalimah* was read. One verse, then two. The past is not erased because it is not a garment to be worn then shorn. It is in the tendrils of hair. The *ruh*. The soul.

A temple is mounted on top of the shrine. A *devi* or goddess alongside a turquoise mosque.

The snake that coils and looks you in the eye so you bow to it.

You bend. A *sajda*. Head to velvet or straw mat.

I offer myself in prayer.

Monkey Man

2001. Monkey Man, *Kala Bhandar,* scours the streets of Delhi at night one summer. This news arrives soon after I leave relatives, renting a small cottage studio apartment in one of Delhi's poshest and cleanest neighborhoods. I am a paying guest in the house of the musician Ustad Vilayat Khan living in Princeton, New Jersey but whose first wife continues to reside in New Delhi. With its singular bed, small round kitchen table and kitchenette, it is a room of my own.

The summer's hot spell is previously unknown to me, a 110 degrees Fahrenheit. Air conditioners are still few and far in between, even in wealthy homes. The cottage has only a ceiling fan. Sweat drips unless we are in shade; even the water from the tank is too warm and a bath provides no relief. There is only partial respite when the sun sets.

When news of Monkey Man arrives, it headlines newspapers and television news. The Monkey Man, half-monkey/half-man, wearing a helmet, attacks people sleeping outside on their own terraces in Delhi slums and resettlement colonies. He steals babies and scars faces.

There is a knock at my door. My cousin, Abid, close in age, has shown up abruptly. "Your mother sent me," he says weakly. "Monkey Man..." He can sense this intrusion into my newfound freedom is not going to go well.

My mother who watches the local evening 6 news about crime in our small Florida town, also views satellite channels that details news in India. In a single conversation, she moves between the happenings on Highway 19 to the recent failure of rains in Haryana and its effect on crops. Today she read about Monkey Man. Of Delhi's twenty million inhabitants, Monkey Man might attack me.

"Well, Monkey Man is not inside," I tell Abid.

"I see that," he concedes.

When I call her, our words furiously trip over one another. "In this entire city, Monkey Man has nowhere else to be but in my apartment!" I had just started a human rights project in a resettlement colony in South Delhi; the cramped quarters of those neighborhoods a far cry from the manicured lawns of where I stay. That morning I listened to the cultural theorist, Ashis Nandy, provide a psycho-social explanation of the fear and mass hysteria behind Monkey Man among the urban poor.

"But, but, but- "

"I live in one of the most protected areas in Delhi. Monkey Man goes to the slums where there are vulnerable people who sleep outside." I am speaking about Monkey Man as if he is real. "Monkey Man is not even real! He's an imaginary construct of criminality that affects low-income residents. An urban legend because it's so hot right now people can't think straight!"

"Monkey Man could get you!" she insists.

"And Abid is going to defend me from Monkey Man!" I feel slightly bad saying this but I cannot imagine the utility of my cousin in this situation.

"No, but he could- "

We argue until the minutes on the SIM card on my

phone run out and I am exasperated at her about that too. Her concern about my safety in India is both real and hyperbolic, expressed through Monkey Man and the dispatch of my helpless cousin.

But what I could not see then and can only admit now is that I am slightly amused; my mother believes in myth as if it is real. And after all, why wouldn't she? She is myth, arising from a history of half-Hindu, half-Muslim, the first of her tribe to immigrate to the United States. And I am myth, once half-Hindu, half-Muslim, tribal-agricultural in background, born in Florida, educated in elite schools, and now returning to India because I close my eyes and see red.

Monkey Man, half-monkey/half-man, as the incarnation of hot summer fears, could be real. Monkey Man could even come to Pandara Road. It is possible too, that for the trouble of his travels, I might actually tell him to sit down at the kitchen table and offer him a cup of tea.

Monkey on the Roof

Delhi

This city is cruel- chaos- unceasing movement. Rooftops blooming with flowers
and trailing vines. The wild everywhere.

August rain floods *barsatis* and basements. An orange bobcat awaits me at the top of the steps. She frightens the house cat who ambles on a thin iron railing on the terrace outside the glass door.

I come home, standing at the base of the stairs, only to find both cats peering at me.

Me, the tenant who watches the wild from birth and the domestic made wild.

We are all made wild here.

IV.

On Language

1983. English words escape me.

After that summer in the *kothi,* during my first year of kindergarten, the English language evaporates into clouds on a flight between New Delhi and Florida. It is not a total loss, but a fragmented one. My linguistic undoing is compounded by watching the 1979 flick *Suhaag,* Rekha in a sari lined with gold circles with Amitabh Bachchan, a red scarf around his neck and bottle in hand, dancing in a room of mirrors, on the VCR at home on incessant replay.

One day I ask my teacher, Mrs. Aimes, for a glass of water in Urdu. Mrs. Aimes dons a dirty-blond bob and wears mid-length skirts. She kneels down to understand me to no avail. Returning to the line, ready to embark on a school trip, I whisper a curse to describe Mrs. Aimes to another classmate, a supposed confidante. The classmate detects I have spoken a bad word, albeit in a foreign language; she tells on me.

Mrs. Aimes calls my parents.

My mother and father apologize, "She spent three months in India last summer."

A few months later, I take a standardized test in a cubicle. The a, b, c answer choices overwhelm me. I am short of breath. Each line crowds into one another as I mark off random choices to fill in the circles. I fail the test, then kindergarten at the year's end.

No one blames me for the failure, the strangeness of losing a language spoken since birth. My father loses his Indian accent even before I am born. His spoken English is impeccable. Sometimes, he recites lines from Dickens or Shakespeare. My mother does not learn English until she comes to America. She gains fluency through the smaller tests of assimilation- buying groceries, passing a driver's license test, making deposits at the bank.

In summer school, I delight in countless pages. Some are illustrated, others plain text. Kids circle the streets with bikes. They run along the seawall to each other's houses. I read, tumbling my way through skies. The books are all in English. Any traces I bear of Hindi, Urdu or Mewati gained the prior summer, playing with nephews on the rooftop, dancing in a circle at a cousin's wedding, are temporarily lost.

My sister, Sabina, born in the village in a room later filled with lentils, no place to sit or lie, only swim amongst green beads, understands the language the best of the siblings. Perhaps it lies in her birth itself; my mother in labor for two days with the help of a midwife. When we should all be asleep, Sabina has late-night conversations with female cousins. She sends them Christmas cards every year written in perfect cursive.

My older brother, Arshad, resembles Mamu Tayyab in height and broad shoulders. He knows only certain phrases. He injects three Mewati words into a string of English sentences spoken with an Indian accent.

The villagers convene and listen to his every utterance.

"The only Urdu word you used in that sentence was 'and'!" I complain.

The villagers nod to one another; they are ready to elect him for political office and place a wreath of marigold flowers around his neck.

He dismisses my comment as jealousy of his charm.

My younger brother knows the least of any Indian language. He responds to every sentence with *acha*, 'okay'. Even as everyone tries to please and baby him, as a little boy, he dreads these trips into the hinterland.

To varying degrees, we all lose our command over our language in those two weeks. Time and place and speech is ruptured. So much is conveyed and we can only understand pieces, as if for those two weeks, we are floating together in a single, starry dream.

During one of these trips, we are not more than teenagers seated around the dining table at the *koth*i. My cousin, Haleema, like many women in my family, speaks non-stop in a series of ongoing reprimands. I only half understand her. Her latest rebuke, pouring chicken curry on my plate and handing me a large roti, is that we, the American children, should learn Mewati.

"No one says that she or my other relatives should learn English," I complain to my mother.

Years later, I do not mind; it is the scolding of *apna-pan*, one's own. To know another language is to open a portal into another world.

She is claiming her right over my tongue.

Family trips to India become less frequent, giving way to the busyness of school, friends and life. In college, when I enroll in C.M. Naim's Urdu course, my relatives and my parent's friends inquire why.

"It will yield no money or marketable skills," Mamu Tayyab tells my mother over the telephone. "She should study economics or finance instead."

"Of course, he will think that," I groan.

Until college, I do not appreciate that our family possesses its own dialect. Which of the three languages- Hindi, Urdu or Mewati- is my mother speaking?

During my first stint in India after college, my nieces and I sit around in the courtyard. They find my continued presence odd but welcome it. I allow them to keep me abreast of the latest popular culture happenings. Their schooling covers the range of elementary, middle and high school English medium schools. When they see me copy down vocabulary from the newspaper to learn Hindi, India's national language, they parse the sentence for me. Sometimes, they know the English word. Often, they string together a Hindi phrase to describe my word in question.

I ask them too about Mewati. "*Naaj ka bhai?* What does that mean? Mom always uses it."

"Brother of grain," they laugh. They shake their heads. "She doesn't mean it literally. It's just a…" They nod as if I should just know, "a saying."

And *'humbe'*? I ask.

All three giggle uproariously.

When the women get together in their knitting circle, my aunt says *'humbe'* with force. I too know that it means something like 'right on' or 'that's right'.

We tape each other in Mewati. We shriek at the replay. We record my bhabhi, their mother, speaking in English. We correct her pronunciation and awkward tying of phrases.

My bhabhi frowns. She holds my hand and complains, "If only I could learn English! You teach me!"

Each of us wants the language we do not have.

To know India, I am convinced, is to know its languages. I feel five years old again as I seek out one tutor after another. An editor of a Hindi worker's newspaper, *Faridabad Majdoor Samachar*. A retired tenth grade Hindi teacher who instructs me to read bus signs, street signs, newspaper clippings and children's books like the comedic stories of *Akbar and Birbal*. I write Hindi Devanagri script, derived from Sanskrit, a series of lines, coiled letters, and hooks.

Devanagri script

A retired 10th grade Urdu teacher teaches me Urdu script. Derived from Arabic and Persian and developed after Moghul or Muslim rule in South Asia, Urdu is the language of famous couplets and poetry. It is the language most Mewatis adopt before Hindi, if they have not forsaken Indian languages altogether for English. It is the language that Yasin Khan seeks to protect in 1932 when the Raja of Alwar prevents its learning in Mewat schools. In Delhi, I only encounter one line of bookstands in Old Delhi, the predominantly Muslim section city, with Urdu texts. Even its print is ghettoized. The declining state of Urdu is lamented by Indian Urdu scholars, for it is a language of undoubtable *khubsoorati,* beauty, and *nazakat,* delicacy.

Urdu script

And then there is lived life itself.

In those early trips, the last place I want to be for anywhere too long is in an office or among a group of

English speakers. I spend a year in the sprawling slums of Yamuna Pushta in Old Delhi. Each day my head hurts as I traverse between the languages of the street and that of English-speaking intellectuals and artists. It is how I pick up the various registers of the spoken word as I come to know the residents and at the end of the year watch the Delhi government raze down homes in one of its largest gentrification projects. I spend time in an industrial area with workers for Indian and multinational companies who earn below the paltry required minimum wage; we distribute a worker's paper to thousands of daily commuters walking on foot through railway crossings and dusty paths. These hundreds of encounters, confusing and complex, add layer upon layer to my understanding of a changing India.

I receive a spectrum of insults and compliments about my language skills. That I speak like a foreigner, an Indian, a Kashmiri, the Italian Sonia Gandhi. The remarks depend upon whether I am seeped in city streets and sounds on that day. Only over time, when I visit family in Mewat, they finally do say, "Now, you speak just fine. You understand everything." Then, I have been bestowed an award, an emblem of excellence on my lapel that only I can see.

Glossary of Meo Terms

Kaha Ho Go (not seriously happened)
Koi Baat Naa/Koi Na (nothing serious, leave it)
Bao- wind
hun- yes
hoon/hoonlu/unghe/unghlu- there
heen/heenlu/inghe/inghelu- here
makhi- fly
karkehani- having done
lekarhani- having taken
ae wari- oh friend
took/kalen/roti- food
sanjku/samlu- evening
dhere/dherai- morning
dhooparlu/dhooparku- noon
dhooparpachhe/dindaleh- afternoon
khat/charpai- cot
goodri- mattress

Footsteps

In 1932, the leader of the Communist Party of India (CPI) arranges for a meeting in its Connaught Place office between Yasin Khan and Mohandas K. Gandhi.

In 2003, seventy-one years later, I find myself in that same office, searching for the biography of Mohammad Ashraf, a partial Meo and active member of the CPI.

I cannot remember if I have a title. Do I just utter his name?

A man takes me through the book stacks; he knows immediately which text I am seeking. A group of men are huddled in a corner, eating their lunches of rotis and vegetables out of tin tiffins. I receive the book of hardback gray binding with cupped hands like I am gathering flowers or seeds.

Only I am not ready for its contents. I do not open it for another ten years.

Years later, I learn that Yasin Khan once visits this same office. I wonder if we walk through the same book stacks. If we see the same circle of men in thin collared shirts and gray slacks, eating their lunch, discussing politics.

In 1932, Yasin Khan oversees crowds of Muslims in protest against the Raja of Alwar at Jama Masjid, India's largest mosque. Thousands are seated, standing, sleeping on the dozens of steps that lead to this sanctuary's three gates, four towers and forty-meter-high minarets of red sandstone and white marble. The protestors occupy Jama Masjid for days, like young American activists would later occupy Wall Street. They challenge the Raja of Alwar's discriminatory policies. They term the journey from their homes to the Jama Masjid a *hijrat,* a migration that is also an exile.

In 2003, seventy-one years later, I visit the Jama Masjid. I spend whole afternoons there, often alone. I talk to strangers, small groups of women, an old widow. I pray. Through the latticework, I gaze at the hypnotic streets of Old Delhi where cycle rickshaws abound, slaughtered meat hangs in alley stores, and covered women haggle for jewelry and scarves. Women whisper in the ladies' section of this mosque. Children play in the pool of water for ablution in the center of this monument.

I do not know this until now, but again, our footsteps must have met.

Steps of the Jama Masjid

A Changing Gurgaon

In the years to come, with a deluge of foreign capital, Gurgaon changes at a dizzying rate. New five-level malls, multiplexes, call centers, eateries, high rises, corporate headquarters, factories. With its sheen new structures and labor unrest, some call it the next Dubai. Farmers become overnight millionaires through real-estate speculation.

Family stay at the *kothi* but many complain about its location in the old part of Gurgaon, less the literal center of Yasin Khan's household. My younger cousins, nieces and nephews eagerly ask am I impressed with the new golf course; if they have malls like this in America.

I overcome shame by going deep into my history, as if the weight of history lies on my shoulders themselves. A shame that comes from listening to others disparage this place, ignorant of the hues and reflections of complex land, or who can only cast pity on forgotten territory that still offers a trailing sense of home. My younger relatives overcome shame through openness to a rapidly changing India, leaving behind the past, a glance behind the shoulder. In our cultural universes, I am less distant from my younger cousins. Yet some part of me will remember earlier days when we struggled to speak to one another, piecing together awkward bits of English, Urdu and Mewati, as if we were finding ways to tumble towards one another. I enjoyed our mismatch of worlds.

The interior of Mewat, however, remains largely the

same. My relatives will, in pieces, move out and undertake complex commutes to raise their children outside of it.

In 2008, Mamu Tayyab passes away, an unexpected heart attack in the night. He returns from a wedding and late that night suffers chest pains. No one suspects its seriousness. He dies before he reaches the hospital on the staircase of the *kothi*.

I have just returned from Florida when my mother's phone call of cracking tears informs me about his death in the parking lot of Newark airport. "And you're coming with me to India for his funeral," she says. She has never quite forgiven me for my arguments, silent and spoken, with Mamu Tayyab. "He cared for you," she often repeated. Once she shows him my business card from my legal aid job which she carries in her wallet. Mamu Tayyab says that I bear affinity to my grandfather, Yasin Khan. Now Gurgaon, bereft, is a different place. With no patriarch to hold all the disparate pieces of this large family together, there is less fear, less concern.

I wait to see the rest of Mewat explode into another landscape entirely.

Gurgaon-I

Gurgaon-II

Kahain Loo (Where are you?)

2010. I return to India, a lawyer with a one-way ticket, and join an Indian human rights organization. I find a way after meeting another lawyer, Sukti, working there at a dinner in New York; her passion is contagious. After a subsequent conversation in Central Park, a hot June day where people wearing as little as possible stroll past fountains, on the way home, I encounter a $20 bill on sidewalk on 7th avenue. *What is the probability of finding money on the street in plain daylight?*

It is a sign. If I too move to India, leaving a legal aid job where I am appreciated and my first apartment with enough room to house a three-seater couch, I should not worry so much about money or financial security; it will come.

Few seem to find this a good idea. No one is surprised.

Some give me a send-off and gift me a blue Afghan necklace; others pick fights or ignore me. It is not until I reach Delhi and wake up one morning, on a spare mattress in a friend's apartment, listening to the sounds of early morning pressure cookers, the intermittent whistle of vegetables and dals being cooked, and watching the sunlight waft into the bedroom, do I feel a lightness in my chest.

In India, I visit relatives intermittently.

One cousin, each time he sees me, uncomfortably asks in Mewati, "*kahain loo?*" *where are you,* a rhetorical question regarding my existential state. When I fail to answer, he lets the question drift into silence. My intention is not to return to Mewat or even to write about it; it feels too daunting a task. Who am I to write a book about a place and a history so complicated and unknown? I am weary too of the questions, concerns, judgements.

Estranged from my writing self as it is, writing poetry occasionally, I follow activism's calling. It is the American recession and Delhi, with its honey of passionate, interesting work is buzzing with expats from all over.

Meos or Minas

Religion was not lost
by the slaughter of the cows.

Religion was not lost
with the eating of white (refined) sugar.

Religion was not lost
when prostitutes' homes were visited.

So tell me how will religion be lost
by the meeting of brothers?
    -Mirasi song

2010. We arrive by train late at night, driving in an auto down a quiet road filled with repair shops and small eateries, finding ourselves, the motor humming as we inquire if there are still rooms available, at the Pinky Hotel, its fluorescent lights ablaze. Later, we are told the Pinky Hotel is a place of disrepute. At the time, we, an Irish activist, a dirty-blond intern from Boston who eventually moves to Alaska, and a long-time Indian health activist, Sanjai, who dons a silver front tooth that glints when he pontificates with a slightly open mouth, are only concerned that it appears clean and the restaurant downstairs serves satisfactory dal tadka after long days in the field.

Our team of lawyer-activists conducts a fact-finding mission after I read of a newspaper account about private doctors performing unnecessary hysterectomies on village women in Dausa, Rajasthan. Time moves quickly as we scour the news for human rights violations and track down plaintiffs. A consumer rights group claims that the hysterectomies are a devious means to make more money.

When we arrive in Dausa, Rajasthan, it is only the end of April but the air is already suffused with a hot thickness and the desert winds are blowing. We drink one bottle of water after another, saving the plastic containers to discard in garbage bins rather than throw on the ground which is common in India. In this small village, a crowd of women share the same story- complaints of stomach pain followed by a doctor's advice to undergo a hysterectomy, the full pulling out of the uterus, instead of another procedure or prescribed medicine. The women seem fractured by their pain but they laugh too, gripping exposed stomachs beneath sari blouses, as they gather around us and relay the story of me too, me too.

The Irish activist is annoyed. "They are not even serious about it."

I speculate that it could be nervous laughter.

A few weeks later, we return, holding camp in a bare room of high walls with our own medical doctor to determine whether the hysterectomy is needed. The doctor consults with sixteen women while I photograph them with my Nikon DSLR for the filing of the petition. Film has given way to digital images, a constant clicking of the camera and looking down to survey the photograph on the viewfinder. Only one may have actually needed a hysterectomy; the rest suffered from poor hygiene.

Our doctor, Dr. Narendra Gupta, having studied abroad, returned to India and now lending his time to such efforts, is from a grassroots public health coalition. He has tender green-blue eyes and a moustache bearing gray strands.

As we eat lunch together, he inquires about my background.

Over the years, I have come to understand that because of my light skin color and pedigree, I appear upper caste or Brahmin Hindu, or elite Muslim, a Pakistani, a Kashmiri. Any possibility but a Muslim Meo living in the Diaspora.

Only the doctor, familiar with Mewat, inquires why I have never chosen to conduct a fact-finding there.

With the weight of my family background and history, I suggest that it is too daunting.

He smiles with knowing. "They are a tough people."

He warns me to be careful in Dausa, Rajasthan. "Private doctors have been known to send thugs. There is some danger to doing this work." That thought never passes my mind until then, reminding me that one of the lawyer's in our office, walking home on the train tracks, was assaulted in the back of his knees with an iron rod.

The doctor explains that the women we interviewed at this camp today belong to the Meena tribe. Meos and Meenas once belonged to the same tribe but Meos slowly converted to Islam and Meenas remained Hindu. Meos are classified as Other Backward Classes in the Census; Meenas are considered Scheduled Castes and Scheduled Tribes. Relatives complain that there is no difference between the two groupings, except that the latter receive reservations or government-endorsed affirmative action schemes.

Earlier that morning, as I click each photograph, looking into the viewfinder to photograph these women in pain that could not be articulated and yet swathed in bursting color, smiling both reluctantly, even accidentally, for the camera, I feel close to them. I did not know that I was coming closer to a sister tribe.

One click, after another, after another.

Each piece, each travel in this country keeps leading me inadvertently back to the past.

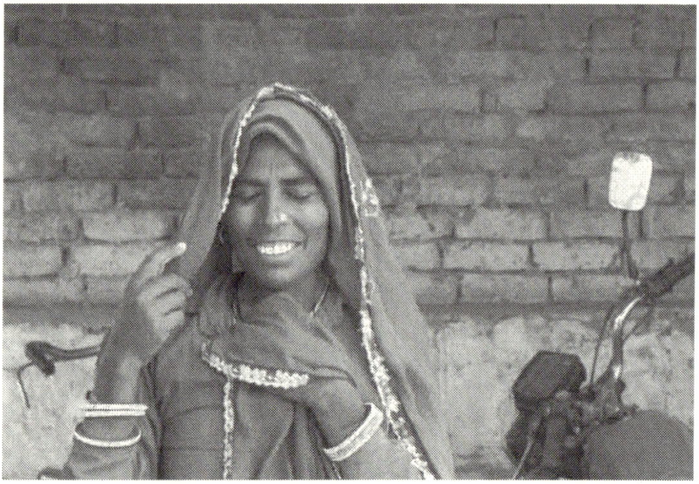

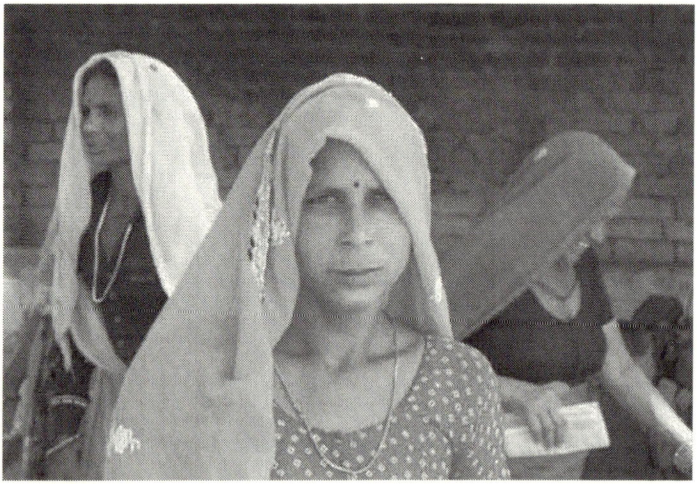

V.

My Bag is Not Full of Bombs

At the airport checkpoint,
my bag is not full of bombs
but books and bangles.
Can they be bombs?

Silver bangles on my wrists,
Beaded neck work.
Are you Kashmiri?
Are you a princess?
Did you pack that bag
all by yourself?

In third grade,
a classmate asks,
do you carry a gun?
I must;
I showed him my prayer rug.

Am I terrorist?
I am a terrorist.
I come from that lineage-
Why do you fault me?

To always wonder
if those around you
Sniff you differently.

On Kashmir

2011. When I read a news account of a fake encounter in Kashmir, I plan a fact-finding investigation there. The Kashmiri army and local police are said to have colluded in the murder of a disabled young man, one of hundreds of "fake encounters," where an innocent is killed under the label of a terrorist.

Upon Partition, Kashmir has been disputed territory under India and Pakistan. Its complex history involves demands by both governments, as well as Kashmiris themselves desiring an independent state. Wrongful killings often do not make their way into news beyond Kashmir, a graveyard of unknown deaths. Yet, this story does.

Our office, with its mess of cubicles and swirling staff has a shortage of toilet paper and the occasional mouse. It continues to brim with activists and seekers looking to funnel conscience into adventure, gain experience through investigations and contentious lawsuits. I am paid far below my pay grade. Dirty and emaciated most of the time, I drastically cut my hair too short in a fit of exhaustion from the summer heat wave. I am not happy but I am closer to being alive; I am closer to my own fire.

"Is it safe there?" I ask Faisal, a local lawyer, over my mobile, standing not too far away from a blue-tiled urinal in the alley near our office. Faisal and I have not met.

"Yes, yes, of course. Come, just come," he replies as

Indians do, a beckoning to his home state akin to a dinner invite.

My colleague Vivek and I set forth on a train journey. Vivek wears glasses too large for his face with a distinct hair part and speaks gently. Vivek used to work with disabled people in a social service agency. New at work, he is befuddled at our seriousness, scourging newspapers for reports of the terrible, our failure at times to break for lunch.

As the train rushes through hills and countryside, Vivek offers one joke after another. The relentlessness of this work at times leads to delirium. Exhaustion ripples into laughter, taking us farther and farther away from Delhi, a city of twenty million inhabitants, extremes of cold and heat, a city constantly turning itself over.

We land in Rajouri countryside nestled between India and Pakistan, a hotbed of supposed terrorist activity, particularly in the 1990's. Our small wooden guesthouse lies on the bank of a stream in the valley. We meet Mr. Bashir, a disabled activist with a white beard, travelling with the help of a single crutch underneath his right arm. He brings us to the community center, a building on the lone road at the beginning of the ascent of the mountain.

I sit amongst a full room of local men, speaking on top of one another about the boy that died and how he is blessed, special. "People disappear all the time and no one notices. This time the reports, the media, this investigation…"

I have grown used to listening to stories in an order

that is not sequential, then controlling and structuring the narrative to comprise an affidavit, a plaintiff's testimony. Finding the constraints of the story is not just an instrumental exercise; it is a literary one.

It feels ironic to interrupt these men, steer the story, command the room. These same men could easily have comprised elders years ago assembled in a family living room. Then and there my role might have been to serve or nod, silent or marginal to a conversation about politics or the world.

Yet, in this moment, on a Rajouri hillside, in a room of community leaders and later on the roadside itself, the sun glinting off the hills, sitting in a plastic chair next to a tea stand where I meet the father because his home is tucked within mountain terrain itself,. Taking his affidavit, I am the one crafting politics.

The Kashmiri Army and police claim the young man they shot in a deserted forest over a period of twelve hours is a prized member of the Lashkar-e-Taiba, a deemed Pakistani terrorist organization. Yet, when the body is brought for burial and local community members clean him, there are questions as to whether he is circumcised. If he is Hindu, the body would not be circumcised. After further investigations, including an autopsy, the conclusion is reached that the young man is a Muslim because of his circumcised penis but no, he is not a member of the Lashkar-e-Taiba. The half of his face that has not been disfigured by bullets suggests that he might be the boy, lost in song, disabled in some way, roaming often and alone, bereft, in the Kashmiri countryside. Most likely, a young man from the Army and his friend from the local Rajouri police, concocted a plan of labelling the disabled boy as a terrorist and shot him in such a way that he is no longer recognizable. Both the young men who carry out the fake encounter are actually Muslims. For the murder of a terrorist, they will receive money and prizes.

Our case is not complete without a trip to the hospital where the postmortem is conducted, and to the police station, further up the mountain alongside a single cascading river where the case has been filed. The officers ask where we are from.

"Human rights," I mumble and offer a head-nod; my answer is self-explanatory. A head nod is most effective in India, encouraging tacit understanding even where this is none.

"Oh, National Human Rights Commission." NHRC is a governmental body. One presumes that other arms of the government have to cooperate with one another. Rather, I work for an independent NGO that refuses to take Indian government funds because it sues the government and issues press releases to publicly shame it.

I smile. It is not a lie if I do not verbally respond.

The officer talks at length, reclining in his chair. He explains a system of rewards for encounters and little monitoring or oversight of what comprises an encounter.

It is a novelty for outsiders to come into these parts; Vivek and I are everyone's guests. Kashmiri hospitality is doled at every turn, including at this police station where information is being given like freshly cut Kashmiri apples.

Tea is brought out in small China teacups. The officers inquire whether I want to see the postmortem video.

I eagerly say yes.

When they turn it on, I am eating a glucose biscuit dipped in chai. The video is almost entirely of their handling of this boy's genitalia to determine if it circumcised.

I nearly choke. "Thank you, that is enough." I say. How uncomfortable to watch this video with these men and yet strangely they do not seem to feel the same discomfort.

"Are you sure?" They reply.

"Yes," I respond. "We should be going."

"But first, you must have lunch."

If we are suing them, how can we eat their food?

"We must have," Vivek does a head nod. "I am starving. They are feeding us with so much love."

"We are not here for their love," I whisper but I am famished too.

They take us upstairs, laid out on a table in silver dishes are plates of rice, a bowl of chicken curry, a yogurt mix of raita, and a petal decoration of sliced apples.

Earlier that trip, Vivek wants to stop and eat. Reminding him that we are not on a holiday, but a fact-finding investigation, I let us pause for samosas and chai.

During that conversation, he asks, "Do you ever feel like you don't belong to India because you are Muslim?" Muslims are India's largest minority.

"I am not even Indian," I reply. Only I do not know that I believe that. "Yes, sometimes."

I tell him the following story, "On a fact-finding, after I finish work on the case, we are invited to one of the homes of the NGO plaintiffs, a consumer advocate who insists on treating us to an ornate Rajasthani thali of food. He tells us that he likes his neighborhood but wants to leave because there are just too many Muslims—they are dirty, they eat off the same plate, they spread tuberculosis..."

Vivek's raises his eyebrows. "Oh no," he says softly.

"I am too stunned to say anything. How would he feel if he knew that he fed this lavish meal to a Muslim? Would he see me as dirty too? When he asks us to sign on a book with our contact info, I only sign my first name. My last name is very Muslim. It means compassionate in Arabic. My intern at the time, a law student from Boston, signs "inshallah" (God willing in Arabic), 'we would all meet again.' Afterwards, I thank her."

Vivek frowns when I tell him this story. While he is in Kashmir, he decides he is no longer Vivek but Shahnawaz, his Muslim alter ego.

I picture him wearing a white topi hat characteristic of traditional Muslim men, especially at Eid prayer.

"We should do a disability project in Northwest Pakistan," he says.

"So, you can go on fact-findings like this?" I surmise.

"Yes! I never thought I would go to Kashmir and here I am!"

Mr. Bashir hobbles through the mountains with greater agility than any of us to guide our group to a candle-lit dinner in another activist's home that evening. The women remind me of relatives, largely shrouded, bringing plates of never-ending food.

Mr. Bashir asks me where my family is from. When I tell him Mewat, he praises the religiosity of its people. With the growth of the Tablighi Jamaat, Mewat is now known far more for strains of religious conservatism. Mewat bears some resemblance to the history of Kashmir. Both places have pasts of Hindu-Muslim syncretism, largely harmonious interpolated communities that went through radical violence during British colonialism and Partition. Radical extremism grew roots. Constant tousles with the government render them both areas that anyone with a little bit of education chooses to leave.

Only Kashmir is stunning and gentle and Mewat is no longer after mining, deforestation and the growth of gangs. I can adopt Kashmir as a second home.

"Can I buy land here?" I ask the driver later, kneeling forward into the front seat. Along the side of the road, water rushes through the valley's rocks. The sky above is only white and blue, swirling clouds in a bright clear sky, lacking the murky greys of Delhi smog. "It's so beautiful, why would anyone want to leave?"

"If you are not Kashmiri, you cannot buy land. That is the law."

I am disappointed. I too want a house in Kashmir next to a rolling river.

When we leave Rajouri, we make our way to the capital of Srinagar, driving on Moghul Road, still under construction and not officially cleared by the government. Only I trust these drivers as I have come to trust strangers during these fact-findings, relying less on what is deemed acceptable, more on my own gut.

Occasionally, we stop to take pictures, each vista more beautiful than the last. Tall green trees on mountain tops. Faint blue-grey mountains dotted with sheep and horses. Hanging off the side of the mountain like a delicate earring, a faraway *sarai* or resting place that King Akbar, a Mughal emperor, builds in the 1500's lies in the distance. I imagine in those days, caravans of hundreds of people traveling for days, lost in time.

Not far away from the summit of the mountain, there is a Sufi shrine. Visitors clasp hands and make a prayer before a modest green structure for the grave lined with small, flapping silver flags. Afterwards, we are given free pink tea or kahwa to drink in tiny earthen bowls.

When we arrive in Srinagar, we check into the hotel and sign in our names. I put down Delhi as my home location. Under nationality, I write down U.S. citizen.

We meet Faisal, the young lawyer, for tea. "You should not have indicated that you are American." He seems concerned but not apologetic.

"You never told me that!" I am irritated for the lack of warning, the damage done.

"That other guy from your office, the British one, he

was walking all around Srinagar taking pictures." He is referring to the white British photojournalist; Kashmiri authorities asked him to quietly leave the country.

I am of the soil, friends say. Still, I am nervous.

"It will be fine," he says.

Faisal tells us how there are few civil society groups allowed in Kashmir at all to protect people. It is not difficult to see why so little news of this place ever reaches mainstream news. To do such work is inherently dangerous.

The next morning at 9 a.m., there is a hard knock on the door. Men in uniform and dangling guns stand before me.

"Where are you from?" The army man asks.

Vivek's room is across from mine. Already interrogated, he is transfixed at the doorway, frightened.

"From Delhi, of course." I do not say anything else; I have no paperwork to prove that either.

They nod.

Vivek breathes in relief. We do not speak further about the Army's visit.

Faisal insists that we see the sights of Srinagar. The night before he drives us around Dal Lake and to the Hazratbal shrine. When we visit temples and shrines, there are checking points throughout and yet none of them asks for identification. The checking done less for actual security than intimidation. In Srinagar, there are eyes watching everywhere. In this city filled with armed men, the mood is suspicious.

Yet again as we travel around the gardens of Kashmir, how can one not be transfixed by the beauty of this city? Indeed, all the hard and stressed places wash away into a multitude of roses and bubbling fountains. Vivek asks me to take pictures of him near a flower bush in Nishad Garden. Most everyone I know has never been to wondrous Kashmir. I want to tell everyone that I have been to this place; everyone should come to this place.

We leave Kashmir that night on a shared van back to Jammu, speeding through the night sky. Sitting next to the window, an irresistible urge to vomit overcomes me. I lean outside the window, puking along the Jammu-Kashmir highway. The van stops for a few minutes and standing along the side of the road, I continue to vomit the day's food. I know this is more than car sickness; I have let the fear pass through me.

Vivek says, "Car sickness. It happens," and pats my back.

We file a case of human rights abuses against the Kashmiri army and police in the highest state court of Kashmir, the Srinagar High Court. Three years later, a High Court judge issues an opinion in our favor. My favorite line, akin to poetry, about the mere absence of recognition of the death itself, is "Gone are the days, when the people on noticing the murder, would say the sky has turned red." The men who staged the fake encounter are dubbed parasites and vultures. By then, I have moved out of Delhi and read the opinion from my office in Edison, New Jersey. I do not learn whether and how the decision is implemented. I flinch though at the judge's use of "mentally retarded" in the decision. Still, it is a startling win.

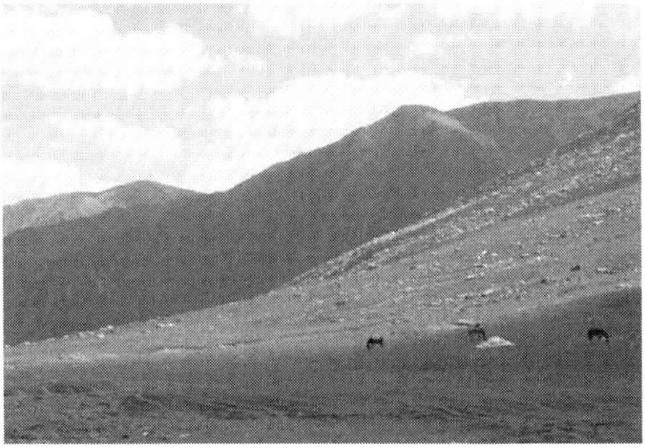

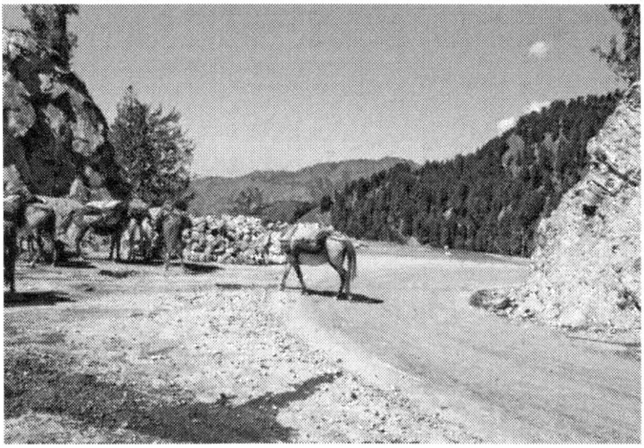

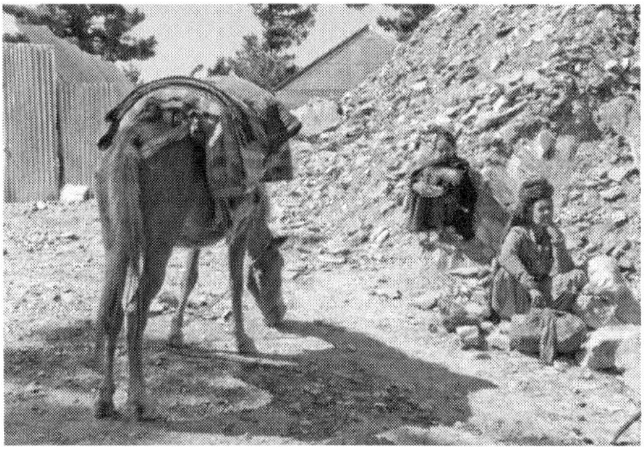

Excerpts from the Srinagar High Court's Decision, April 2014

1. All norms of humanity when breached in the lust of getting favours, humanity gets buried. Allegedly SP Noor Hussain and Sepoy Abdul Majeed dubbed a mentally retarded man as a terrorist, then staged a fake encounter and brutally killed him so as to earn cash reward and compensation.

2. Article 21 of the Constitution of India, guarantees right to live with dignity, never recognized inhuman and degrading treatment. Allegedly killing of a mentally retarded person, in a manner it has been is totally violative of Article 21 of the Constitution. Gone are the days when the people, on noticing the murder, would say that the sky has turned red. Such was the belief and value for the human beings.

3. Can the persons, who allegedly have staged a fake encounter and killed a mentally retarded person, be termed as human beings. Can't they be termed to be parasites, vultures and ferocious animals. Will killing of an innocent person allow such persons to remain in peace by earning promotion or cash reward. The mentally retarded person deserved treatment and protection, alas: an SPO and Sepoy allegedly, in greet to get awards and promotion, have killed him brutally.

4. The brutal killing of mentally retarded person required an in-depth inquiry and investigation. Noticing

the tardy pace, instant petition has been filed seeking writ of Mandamus so as to command the respondents to investigate the matter and present challan against the accused persons in the court of competent jurisdiction and thereupon direct speedy trial. It is also prayed that a special investigation team of CBU shall be constituted to conduct an impartial investigation.

VI.

Finding Rimbaud

A few months after Kashmir, I find myself in Harare, Ethiopia.

Harare is a Muslim holy city that resembles Old Delhi with its large gates, dozens of alleys and a white-baked mosque in the center of the town. Women wear colorful hijabs and sell vegetables on clothes laid on the pavement. There is even the Alley of Reconciliation where if one meets one's enemy, both persons must declare truce to one another.

My human rights project runs parallel to a similar one in Nigeria where I am invited for a conference. I have never been to Africa. I do fret but conclude it would be absurd not to make the trip. I decide that I must backpack through Ethiopia on my return to India. Knowing nothing about the country except what *Lonely Planet* shares with me, I feel strangely safe as I get down from buses at towns without always a clear idea of where I will stay or eat.

In Harare, I spend a few nights at a guesthouse, a converted eighteenth-century home, where the walls are colored with painted flower ceramic dishes. The owning family overbooks the place on a daily basis. A young girl Aisha, no more than ten years of age, is the only one in the family who knows English and serves as an interpreter. Each morning there is a frantic reshuffling and sometimes travelers sleep on the living room diwan.

At breakfast over honey pancakes and tea, I meet an

adventurous Indian engineer who will watch volcanoes erupt on New Year's Day, a London businessman who sold his house and has been traveling on his motorcycle for two years, and a young British couple, very much in love, who teach English at a university in Dubai.

Ethiopia is off the beaten track and Harare is its most exquisite stop.

Beyond the Alley of Reconciliation and local Sufi shrines, there lies the Rimbaud Museum. At age sixteen, in Florida, I see a film about the bohemian Parisian life of Rimbaud, played by Leonardo DiCaprio before he becomes a sensation. Afterwards, I read Rimbaud's poetry, alongside Neruda and Nikki Giovanni, and wonder about his last painful days in the especially remote, dusty town where he moves to trade in coffee beans and arms.

"I know the skies bursting with lightning,
    and the waterspouts
And the surf and the currents; I know the evening,
And dawn as exalted as a flock of doves
And at times I have seen what man thought he saw!"[1]

More than twenty years after I read his poem "The Drunken Boat," I am wandering through the rooms of his house filled with red and blue stained-glass windows and fragile wooden floors. Here, he underwent his sad, self-imposed exile from Paris and poetry. He stops writing poetry at age 21. He does not live very long either and dies at 37. In his photographs of his last years, he has a short moustache and looks cold and closed off, a bizarre colonialist. He may be heartbroken after his poet-lover Verlaine shoots him in the foot during a drunken fight but still, I am disappointed by this trajectory.

Had he written all that he had to write?

Had he given up?

Had his genius been spent or was he just beginning?

Did he not miss the act of writing?

"You have to write a book," Sukti, my lawyer friend from New York, says to me months ago on a summer bus ride to the Himalayas one weekend. We can see the fork in the road. We are planning grand futures; after all we have seen, to not do so is akin to cowardice.

I intimate ideas that I have about a book. "So far, I have not written a single word," I share.

"We have been making this up all along," she says. The fact-findings, the condemnatory petitions, the jagged professional trajectories.

There is no greater place to write than from a point of experimentation.[2]

In Ethiopia, I carry a notebook. On this trip, I have more time than I have had in years. To think, write postcards, sleep, read novels. Some days I do not see any sights at all, staying inside to read. I begin to scrawl notes for a book about Yasin Khan.

'Amriki' (The American)

Asma, my niece, ten years younger than me, lives near Jamia Millia University in a Muslim neighborhood in Delhi. Her parents, like my parents, are still rooted in Mewat, even if the externalities of their daily existence belong to a new world. Even Delhi, only sixty kilometers away, constitutes the new world. I visit their home often; each time I am ensured a feast.

At first, I telephone and ask, "Are you there today? I might be able to come over."

Then Asma begins to phone me, "Are you coming today? We are going to make biryani and kebabs." If I do not see her for many days, she pouts, "Just wait and see what I do to you when you arrive!" Her threats translate to even more food spread out on a paisley tablecloth on the bed where I sit cross-legged. I await heaping plates of biryani, shami kebabs, homemade coriander and tamarind chutneys. Asma pours portions onto my plate, insisting that if I do not eat, it means that I do not like her cooking.

"Of course, it's very good and of course, I like it," I say with a stuffed mouth.

"Even the yogurt is homemade," she says. Everyone needs an Asma in their life.

In exchange for Asma's generosity, I bring her books, Asma writes Urdu in perfect calligraphy, and I treat her to lunch at the famous Kareem Hotel in Old Delhi, the only place that serves saffron and cardamom flavored sheermal *roti.* When we meet, I share pictures of places most recently traveled. Asma refers to me as a female Ibn Battuta, the medieval Islamic scholar known for his wide travels. In thirty years, he travels most of the Islamic world and the Far East and pens an account of his journey, *A Gift to Those Who Contemplate the Wonders of Cities and the Marvels of Traveling.*

During my many visits, I encounter Asma's father, Zakir, fluent in Persian and Urdu, a senior translator for the National Archives. Only Zakir is unassuming and incomprehensible in person because of his slurred speech and trailing sentences.

His wife, Haleema, my cousin, raises her palm for emphasis, "Everyone thinks he's a fool. They see him and they can't believe that he translates big, important texts."

Zakir calls me *Amriki,* meaning 'the American'. One day he begins to mumble to me at length. I gather stray words here and there. "Palestine," "Human Rights," "Hypocrisy."

I think, but do not say, as the heat rises in my brain, the following: Is he telling me that given current and previous US foreign policy, it is hypocritical of me as an American to come to India and do human rights work here? I understand the argument but I did not even initiate a political conversation with him.

Why am I always struggling to be authentic?

As we make a road trip to Mewat together, our argument continues along Sohna Road. Zakir has a kind face, a prominent beard and a paunch as do many married men in my family. Yet, during that car ride, I want to stick a needle through his arm.

I interrupt him with counterarguments about global human rights and violations in India. I hate resorting to these rough comparisons but I do. "It is not only the US that violates human rights. See what is happening here?" The conversation is ironic as we travel through Mewat which ranks below national averages on health, literacy, clean water, and the environment.

After that day, Asma still insists I come to her house. Even if we argue, we are family.

"Bhai Jaan," how she refers to Zakir, "and his father argue for hours at a time. They only take breaks to pray."

"Doesn't the value of the prayer dissipate if they are arguing the rest of the time?" I ask Asma.

"Bhai Jaan is a fool," Asma repeats her mother's words.

Zakir stands at the threshold of the inner doorway of the room where I am seated awaiting biryani and kebabs.

If I am going to eat not merely as an act of consumption but an expression of devotion, I do not want to be distracted or boiled up about Zakir's flawed anti-imperialist politics.

Asma and Haleema are positioned on both sides of him. "Don't you come inside!" Haleema yells at him. "You let her eat first and not bother her with your nonsense politics."

"Fine, fine, let her eat." Zakir motions an assent with a turn of his palm upwards.

He has recognized my humanity; I appreciate his mercy.

"You go in the other room!" Haleema continues, "We'll bring your food there. Bothering her with your nonsense. She'll stop coming if you don't be quiet!" Haleema continues to yell at him. Asma pushes him out of the room with a thud on his back.

"Bhai Jaan is the biggest fool," Asma repeats when she returns. She sighs and puts another shami kebab on my plate. "Who needs television for entertainment," Asma says, "when we have this?"

Weeks later, Zakir and I speak about Meo history as I shyly reveal my intention to write a book. Me, an American, an *Amriki,* an outsider, an interloper. He gives me a copy of his essay on Meos in the Mughal era, titled "Delhi, Meos and the Great Uprising: A Study of Anti-British Resistance during 1857." I read it and underline portions. I cite him in these pages.

In the sharing of his words, we reconcile.

The Silk Route

2012. A tour of Uzbekistan. My parents enjoy traveling, especially to countries with a history of Islamic significance, and why traverse the Silk Route of Tashkent-Samarkand-Bukhara.

The architecture is opulent, distinct in scope and color. Mosques bear enormous domes in a symphony of turquoise and Persian blue. Mausoleums are studded with green gemstones and gold work. These are cities bearing traces of bazaars, caravanserais, canals, gardens and water fountains. They convey a triumph of aesthetics and the enormity of grandeur and empire.

I too learn about the long arc of Meo history. I summarize and subject my knowledge to my father on the tour bus before we arrive at the government museum in Tashkent.

"Meo derives from the term "Mewasati" which means men of the mountain passes," I read aloud.

"'Mev' also means a hiding place for robbers, a term used in the Indo-Persian court chronicles and British records. Meos may have first entered the northwestern provinces. Some believe that Meos are not Kshatriyas but originally tribes from central Asia. Meos are first mentioned in written history during the time of Prithviraj Chauhan in the 12th century when the first conquests in Mewat begin. Before the attack by Shahabuddin Ghauri in the 13th century, it is said that the entire area between Delhi and Ajmer is Mewat." [3]

I stop here. To think that much of Delhi was once Mewat is mind-boggling. How did I never know this?

My father half listens to my summation, some or all of which he knows, distracted by his own reading. My father has a photographic memory. He is devouring the history of Uzbekistan from the guidebook which he will later recite back to the tour guide speaking at the front. Mewat is of the past and Uzbekistan the vivid present. *Only what if the two converge?* The tour bus halts at the government museum in Tashkent.

We stand in the lobby, staring at paintings of rulers who invaded Mewat. My mother and I, located some distance away from the tour group, peruse large paintings underneath a crystal chandelier.

"There is Babar," I whisper to my mother. "He stole a lot of Meo land."

Babur in his memoir, *Baburnama,* writes,

"The Sultans of Hind, whether from the extent of their territories, from want of opportunity, or from obstacles posed by the mountainous nature of the country had never subdued Mewat. They had never been able to reduce it to order and obedience as was tendered to them."[4]

Only Babar, unlike previous sultans, is successful in his war against the Meos. He defeats Hasan Khan Mewati, a Muslim who marries a Meo woman, who dies during battle against Babar. Hasan Khan Mewati's family is said to have ruled over Mewat for a hundred and fifty years. Hasan Khan Mewati is the last chieftain over Mewat until my grandfather Yasin Khan.

Only Babar, with his deep-set eyes and well-trimmed beard captures my mother's attention. She stares and blinks as if she is flirting with his picture.

"He is very handsome," she says. "Take my picture with him."

I relent; so what if he is of the line of our ancestors' oppressors?

My Mother and Babar in Tashkent

We make our way outside into the center of Tashkent. There stands a statue of Tamerlane, or Timur the Lame, who was actually disabled but history erases these details. He too burned plains of Mewat. His sculpture has him valiantly on a horse in mid-air in the center of Tashkent above a circular array of steps.

Again, we take more pictures.

Facing the Tomb of
Abdul Rahim Khan

2012. Living in various apartments throughout Delhi, at least six separate residences, I learn the obscure streets and sights of this megacity.

Few places in the world are as chaotic as Delhi. Streets end abruptly, stray dogs linger and a bicyclist veer around the corner. Buses fling themselves across highways. Cars honk without purpose and with restless habit. Shrines and temples emerge suddenly. The past and present are always speaking to one another.

Hawkers walk open streets and stores of every kind line the pavement. A woman with a pink nose ring asks pedestrians to buy fruit- mangoes, bananas, lychee. Crumbling monuments gaze at the city with mournful eyes of abandonment and admonition.

My last apartment is a barsati, or a converted rooftop apartment in Nizamuddin West, one bedroom with a small kitchen and garden on the outdoor roof. Once servant's quarters, barsatis are less expensive apartments often rented by artists. The writer Arundhati Roy too once lives in a barsati in the Nizamuddin neighborhood.

This is the first apartment I rent solely on my own, a lease in my name. It is difficult to rent as a single woman, a lawyer, a Muslim. I am given parameters on who may come and go to the apartment. I am asked in detail about my work and purpose here. Few want to rent to anyone falling under these three categories.

During the monsoon, my barsati drips with rain; books get slightly wet and musty in the month of August. Each pitter-patter can be heard. The streets flood with the exorbitant rain. Children play during those torrential downpours. The monsoon is an invitation to be soaked, drenched in new waters.

Nizamuddin Rooftop

My neighborhood Nizamuddin West consists of dozens of alleys.

One section is full of multi-storied wealthy homes.

A short walk away lies the Mughal architecture and gardens of Emperor Humayun's tomb of the sixteenth century.

Another short walk in the opposite direction past shopkeepers selling deep-fried sweets in newspaper bags lies the home of the dargah or mausoleum of Hazrat

Nizamuddin Auliya, a Sufi saint. He belongs to the same Chishti Sufi order as Yasin Khan and my great grandfather, Wali-ji.

A walk to the shrine requires taking off one's shoes to enter the complex down a series of marble steps with a wicker plate of rose petals and incense in hand.

In that same complex lies the grave of Amir Khusrao, the Urdu scholar, poet and musician. He is a disciple of Hazrat Nizamuddin Auliya and the father of the *qawwali*, the devotional music form of the Sufis.

Often, I sit near these graves, soaking in the *qawwalis* sung at sunset by live musicians.

From my roof, I see a smaller tomb glowing in the distance. As I begin to write this book of fragmented history and poetry, I am living in a barsati facing the tomb of a Meo descendant. I do not know it then and learn years later that my apartment faces the tomb of Abdul Rahim Khan who bears almost the exact name as my father, Abdur Rahim.

Emperor Humayun married a Meo woman and asked his minister to marry her sister. The minister gave birth to Abdul Rahim Khan. When Abdul Rahim Khan worked in King Akbar's court, the King was planning to invade Mewat. Abdul Rahim Khan advised the King against it for the Meos are a worthy foe.

Amidst the street sounds and calls for prayer, the tomb is a faint dome of light.

On that rooftop filled with my landlady's herbal plants, I begin to write these pages.

I host dinner parties. Modest gatherings where friends sit on bamboo chairs on the terrace to eat pizza or kebabs. We talk about politics and romances and the future. I can see the guards below who watch the streets and residences trying to peer above but we are too high for their intrusive eyes. I walk barefoot on the terrace; the open sky is ours. I fall in love, a glowing firefly. I fall in love when I first come to India after college, months after I graduate from the University of Chicago. I fall in love again as I begin to write this book. After the relationships end, the scent lingers. One relationship propels me towards India; the other sparks a return to the US.

Abdul Rahim Khan who lives from 1556 to 1627 is known for his poetry, famous dohas or couplets. The most famous of his couplets is one that my own father recites to us many times as children;

> The thread of love, once snapped,
> forever bears a knot–
> *Rahiman dhaga prem ka, mat todu chatkai,*
> *Tootey phir se na milay, milay gaanth padi ja*

Peacock

Thin, wiry feet crush leaves in the spinach garden
skin velvet blue.
Could it be that I could be its skin.
Lizard in the courtyard licks to taste the air.
Bells shake on the dancer's ankles.
The forest is silent at first
but when she wanders, she dances.
Leaves, dirt, and bells.
Dance changes when she sees the peacock f
   or the peacock has a dance too–

is this the only dance that should be seen
and requires listening

The slow turning away of the bird
   who retires for the afternoon.
The dancer's hands are vines that curl and caress.

One spin, three spins, eight-point turn.
Beauty winces at the beauty of longing,
what is folded beheld inside the feathers.

Adopt the turning of the peacock,
and the eyes that are not afraid.

Anarkali (c. 1615)

The sculptor wants an apsara,
human fairy of clouds and water,
in the center of the King's palace.
He relies on my contours. I stand utterly still.

Me, Anarkali, a courtesan in King Akbar's court.

The Prince enters the courtyard,
whispers of slave girls
and courtiers ripple through corridors
signaling his arrival.

The sculptor says,
"Here, here, she is."

I am an image to bow down to on soft knees.

The Prince exits; I break my pose,
flecks of bronze fall at my feet.

~

That night I dress
in a red choli, a gold silk skirt.
A pearl circular nose ring graces my upper lip.
I dance for the King, the Queen, the Prince.

I am gopi Radha
spinning for Lord Krishna,
rendering art with my feet,
the sleight of my veil,
the sway of my skirt.

Prince Salim sends for me.
A thin passageway of water
runs through the palace,
connecting our worlds.

We meet
underneath a shaded banyan tree.
The first rusted leaves
of spring fall over the two of us.

I am living the brightest hues
of the sky before the rain.

~

The King learns of our affair.
His cheeks enflamed,
His son, heir to the empire,
entertains a slave girl,
and calls it *love*!

The King invites me to perform,
I spin red fifteen times in a room
studded with mirrors and sing,

"Where there is love,
how can there be fear?
Pyar kiya to darna kya?
When no veil exists between humans and the divine,
what veil can there be between humans?"

Haunted, the King throws me in the palace dungeon.

~

The King speaks of the divine
but there is none in his heart!
The Prince prepares to battle,
raise swords.

In the gallows, the King vows
to bury me between the palace walls,
even if my dancing bells
will be heard always.

the King will kill the Prince too,
is not the sanctity of the empire his true son?

I propose to so tenderly

carry out a betrayal against the Prince
to save his life and mine.

The sky breaks.

~

In a final reunion,
I wear a white gown
surrounded by a circle of dancers.
I too feign that this is the King's grand acceptance
not a splitting, a departure, a trickery.

I sit across from the Prince,
and do not speak, only gaze.
Then I take a white feather
dipped in clear poison,
whisk it across his cheek.

The Prince descends deeply into a short sleep.
When he awakes, I have disappeared.
The Prince assumes my death.

Escaping through the passageway of lower earth,
I emerge in a distant city of blue light.
Here I mourn the Prince's loss,
learn of days that will be long.

Kathak dancer

VII.

Jodhpur, Rajasthan

A year before, at work, we conduct a fact-finding and file a case on behalf of twenty-nine pregnant women who die in a single month in a government hospital in Jodhpur, Rajasthan. It is my first fact-finding.

"Do not hesitate to speak to these families," Sanjai, an activist at our office, says. He has spent many years in the Rajasthan deserts on rural health. "They are in mourning. They will want to talk to you."

We chase down our plaintiffs in the Rajasthan villages.

One widower, Lala Ram, is not at home when we arrive. We get his phone number. We have never met but he takes a bus back home. In the meantime, we go to another home where the women wail against doorways.

We spend the day with clipped phone calls trying to arrange this meeting, "Lala Ram, are you there? We are coming." When we arrive, our sheer urban female presence so odd, we are like meteors that have landed next to the charpoy outside his hut.

He crouches on the floor. It may be a sign of his caste that he does not sit higher up. We crouch too then sit cross-legged. His family, his father, his mother, his wife's family, all gather with children nestled in their laps.

We make impromptu visits only to find health facilities either closed or barely functioning. Some beds still have smeared blood. We click photographs at each turn, a relentless documentation of negligence and apathy. We sue the hospital and multiple government agencies for these deaths.

In the few days that we are there, we are a flurry of activity. On the last day, when we are in the government hospital, I use my scarf to cover my nose because of the stink.

For months afterwards, Lala Ram calls me in Delhi. I do most of the talking and tell him to wait for the court date. I tell him to contact the local lawyer. I ask him about his family. In India, people often call one another from time to time to say hello, without clear purpose. I find his phone calls endearing until they die down over the passage of months.

When I happen to be in Florida, the case is reported on the front page of a section in the *Wall Street Journal*. My father wakes me up with bed tea and the newspaper.

"See what is in the paper today?" he says, seated next to me.

His enthusiasm surprises me.

My father often recounts that he is one of thirteen children but eight of his siblings die soon after birth. The causes of death are vague or forgotten. Until this case, meeting the men whose wives die in childbirth, I know little about infant mortality, the precariousness of life itself. At the NGO office, I do not tell anyone this fact about my family for I cannot fathom it either. Perhaps, in my messy trajectory, my father sees a full circle, an illumination of the moon.

An American Meo

"Only a journey without a return ticket
can save us from family, blood
and small-town thinking."
  —Dany Laferriere, *The Enigma of the Return*

In 1969, my parents immigrate to the United States as the first American Meos. My father makes the initial, unknown journey at a time when Meos do not leave the region, much less the continent, two oceans away. For decades, my parents are the only Meos in the US. Few relatives visit, denied American visas for even a short stay.

One of the largest Muslim populations in South Asia, around ten million people in India, Meos do begin to leave Mewat and its surrounding areas for less familiar terrains. A growing Meo diaspora, a stream of migrants, although in small numbers, challenge the singularity of my parent's status. One now hears of Meos in the UK and in Australia and even Latin America as members of the family secure visas and employment abroad.

We know and hear of my father's struggles. "I walked two miles to school," he would begin. As children, we moan when he tries to recount his story. Our minds trail off, unable to hold the breadth of his experiences. After living in India, the uniqueness of my father's story becomes evident to me. My father too begins to pen his biography with his limited typing skills. He craves his story be read by future generations.

A Birth and No Name

My father is born in a village called Nai Nangla in Mewat. The village is named after one of our great grandfathers and called Naru Nangla. Whether the name is distorted from Naru Nangla to Nai Nangla or that it once was a residence of barbers (Nais) is not clear. It is a small village with a population of about two hundred and sixty to seventy households. At his birth, there is no school, hospital, or even shops and roads.

My father's birth is a mystery. My grandparents have thirteen children. Eight of the children die either after birth or from childhood diseases like pneumonia or dysentery. The infant mortality rate is very high and there are no nearby medical facilities. When another boy dies before my father is born, my grandfather loses hope. My father estimates that his birthday is in January 1945 but my grandparents could not recollect such details. My grandmother later says that it is the lunar month of Kartik or Bhado, which my father could not translate into the Gregorian calendar. Because eight of his brothers and sisters die before him, my grandmother pierces my father's ears for good luck. He still bears marking of pierced ears.

The village chaukidar who registers births is illiterate. He has to be informed then travels by foot and bus, a whole day affair. The records at that time too are kept in Urdu which itself becomes a problem. "Because there is no hope for my survival," my father writes, "I am not named for some time." Since no one knows what my father is named after birth or his registered name if any, he is called Hundoo, meaning one who roams the village.

Boy in the Village

Partition

In 1947, during the Partition of India and Pakistan, my aunt is born. At that time, my father is two and half years old and sick with smallpox. In Mewat, I see many faces with smallpox scars, dimples indenting cheeks, but my father's face does not bear them. "I do not remember the horrors of 1947," my father writes. "only that I cry a lot for food since it is hard to come by." My father recalls my grandfather, Qamar Khan, guarding the house with a gun. The family travels from village to village seeking safety.

Childhood

My father attends a religious school where the maulvi reads Quran but does not have much other religious knowledge. "He is not much of a teacher or probably I am not a very good student, because I do not learn much which I now regret," my father writes. "He however, does give me the name Abdur Rahim."

A relative is appointed a primary school teacher in the neighboring village a mile away. Every morning that relative rides his bicycle from his village for about an hour and passes by Nai Nangla to reach school by 8 a.m. He is the only teacher for the school up to the fourth grade.

My grandfather asks if he can take my father with him and teach Quran. It is my grandfather's wish that one of his sons memorize the Quran and become a Hafiz. A Hafiz is salvation for three generations, one in his own, one before and one after. My father manages to read Quran but finds that alone out of place and boring. He is the only child reading Quran while others study the Hindi alphabet and math. He is asked to join the first grade but he has to be enrolled in school and given a date of birth. To register him, he is given an age under his actual age and the birthdate of October 10, 1947.

My father does better than expected in elementary school, finishing four grades in two years. He comes back home with his teacher who naps during the hot Mewat summers and gives my father assignments to keep my father busy. The result is that my father gets ahead and promoted to the next grade.

After elementary school, my father suffers from high fevers and develops malaria.

For treatment, he takes bitter quinine tablets. "This lasts for nine months, at times no hope for recovery and no hope for any further studies," my father writes. "My father and elder brother are very happy that I would tend to the cattles and help with agriculture at home. I hated this type of life but had little hope of getting out of it. This illness might have also stunted my growth." Only my father recovers and does return to school.

AIIMS Medical College

My father's writings detail his struggles and successes to obtain education at a time when it is not popular in Mewat, even for boys, to become educated in secular schools. He succeeds at each step. With much hardship, he graduates from elementary, middle and high school, often studying in boarding schools for long periods, to obtain a college degree and finally entrance into All India Institute of Medical Sciences (AIIMS), India's top medical school where he graduates at the top of his class. The graduates from AIIMS are encouraged to pursue opportunities abroad.

Yasin Khan has his eye on my father for years, one intellect recognizing another. When he is in medical school, Yasin Khan pays him a visit at his dormitory.

They exchange a few words.

My father rushes to make him tea but Yasin Khan leaves.

Soon thereafter, he sends a proposal to my father's family.

At the age of eighteen, my father has an arranged marriage to my mother. They meet on their wedding night. Two years later, they give birth to my sister with the help of a midwife in a room in his village.

"Admission to India's top medical college is not as easy and straightforward." my father writes. "First, seventy students are selected. In that list, I am in the top fifty but then there is an interview process. At that time, I have a desire to serve rural India and I say so. They probably like my answer and I am in the final list. I regret that my statement turned out to be totally untrue. The realities of life changed my course. I was already married and Sabina is born just when I finish medical college. There is no way I could afford to take care of my wife and daughter."

My father decides to take the path of post graduate education in US. That year the ECFMG exam to go abroad is offered in Delhi. But prior, the Indian Government disallows that exam, finding it a brain drain since India is investing and preparing doctors for the United States. In fact, several times this question is raised in the Indian Parliament since the education at AIIMS is the most expensive for India.

"The government however, never thought the stipend for post-graduate education could not sustain anyone who has studied all these years and has a family," my father writes. "A few years later when the students and junior doctors agitate then the government is forced to raise the amount. Had this happened around 1970 the course of my career might have been different."

Instead, my father comes back to Delhi. He passes the

exam with 85th percentile and applies for positions in the US. Meanwhile, he is able to get a job as a house physician. Only he needs a job to make more money than Rs 250 per month. He applies to the Haryana Health department for a job in the civil hospital in Gurgaon but no response. He applies at Hamdard Clinic for a job but of no avail.

As a top graduate from an Indian medical college, he is not able to get job that pays enough for a small family of three. "My pride of being a top graduate from a top medical college of India is totally crushed," my father writes. "This convinces me even more that I did not have a bright future there."

When my father receives a job offer from Mount Sinai Hospital in Philadelphia, he makes temporary plans to move to the United States. His migration is part of a slew of professionals from India under the 1965 immigration bill that abolishes the quota system and recruits talent from non-European countries. Many of my father's classmates also come to the US. Every year, they hold reunions in the US or India.

When my parents first come to Philadelphia, my mother cries horribly. She cannot eat on the plane ride over. My father forces her to have a bite in Paris. Some bread, some chicken. Over time, my mother adjusts to life here. There are pictures of her from those days in saris, her long hair hanging loose. In one photograph, she is laughing in a purple sari with a gold necklace dangling around her neck.

On a large television screen in Florida, we watch old home videos, fragments converted into CDs from those early days. My older brother and sister running around trees in circles. My sister narrating with a microphone in front of Niagara Falls. My mother in the kitchen wearing bellbottoms, slicing birthday cake.

In America, we are all given new selves.

My Father Graduating from AIIMS Medical College

Close to the Land

2012. My father's brother, Uncle Mehmood, only a few years younger, feels differently about Mewat, and therefore India. He is of a different mold, loving India in that romantic Bollywood filmi way that I do. His wife, my aunt, does not grow up only in Mewat, traveling the country with her father who serves in the Army. My aunt bears a distinct reddish birthmark on her face. I learn that she studies Russian literature in college where she hangs out with Delhi leftists and serves on the leadership of the student chapter of the Communist Party of India-Marxist (CPI-M). Her grandfather, Chaudhry Abdul Haye, was also a revolutionary whom I later discover in the archives.

When Uncle Mehmood retires from his position as senior management at Unilever in London, he moves to India and builds a farmhouse in Mewat on ancestral land. He stays there every few weeks. He builds an ornate enclosure around my grandparent's graves. Many graves in Mewat are just heaping mounds of dirt.

One afternoon we attend a Rotary sponsored event in Mewat. Meos are suspicious of polio vaccination campaigns, seeing it as a guise for covert government sterilizations. The conservative clerics in Mewat tell the villagers that the polio drops will lead to barrenness. From the early 1900's, many Muslim communities came under the teachings of Wahhabism. Uncle Mehmood sees the Wahhabi influence as the reason behind school curriculums that fail to incorporate science, in contrast to his own upbringing.

The Rotary members are befuddled.

At the meeting, sitting at a wooden table in front of a small crowd, Uncle Mehmood says, "Bring the clerics from their home to speak at the event regarding their objection."

The message is relayed through men who disappear into nearby residences.

We sit for a good hour and wait for the clerics to arrive.

The clerics do not appear. Instead, their representatives revoke their earlier statement. "It is fine," the representatives concede meekly, "for people to get polio drops."

Cowards. "Well, that was a productive day," I say to Uncle Mehmood.

He laughs, the corners of his eyes gathering in crinkles.

After years of corporate life, Uncle Mehmood revives his passion for agricultural farming and starts a dairy with 76 cows and buffaloes to produce unadulterated milk, a rarity for the area where commercial milk is often mixed with soap to increase its quantity, despite the fact that doing so might lead to illness. At the farmhouse, there is a nearby garden with tomatoes and eggplants and small purple clustered flowers. We spend three days overseeing the farm and visiting relatives. This is land near the very villages where my father sought shelter during the height of Partition. At night, there is only intermittent electricity, the night sky studded with stars, small bits of silver in an absolutely quiet stretch of black. There is the occasional dog barking and the sound of the muezzin from twelve different villages, each voice resounding one after another. He shares Meo history because he loves to talk and of all the places he has lived- London, Amsterdam, Singapore- Mewat is still his favorite.

Here I am born in Miami, growing up on the banks of converted Florida swampland in a three-story house near a canal that spills into the Gulf of Mexico and yet this place of open fields, bare rooms, shrouded people and distant mountains still feels familiar.

Somehow, it is still mine.

A Brief Index of Crops[5]

Cereal crops

bajra (pearl millet)

jowar (sorghum)

makka (maize)

dhaan (paddy)

madwa (ragi)

kodon (kodo millet)

gochani (mixture of wheat and gram)

gojaro (mixture of wheat and barley)

bejhari (mixture of gram and barley)

Cash crops

kapas (cotton)

baar/ganna (sugarcane)

tilhan (oilseed)

neel (indigo)

san (hemp)

masino (opium)

Vegetables

tori (ridge gourd)

baingan (eggplant)

aryia (cucumber)

gajar (carrot)

pyaaz (onion)

shakarkandi (sweet potato)

tarbooz (water melon)

kharbooza (musk melon)

chola (garbanzo)

cheena (common millet)

muli (radish)

ajwain (carom seeds)

tobacco

dhania (coriander)

Pulses

Matki (moth beans)

moong (green gram)

urad (split matpe beans)

Crazy Horse

2013. We travel out West. After months in polluted Delhi, it is a relief to be in pristine, open country, passing herds of bison and vast, sparkling lakes. In South Dakota, we learn about Crazy Horse, a Lakota warrior killed by surprise in battle against the 'new' Americans. The Ziolkowski family devotes their lives and funds to erect a memorial, a rock sculpture akin to Mount Rushmore, that consists of Crazy Horse charging in battle, depicted as half-man and half-horse. The family's mission, they say on their website, is to create a record because history has repeatedly submerged its minorities.

Over lunch, my father and I argue about the history of the Native Americans. He is uncomfortable with their present-day poverty. He and I for as long as I can remember talk about politics. When we do this, my mother says we are like the t.v. political commentator, George Stephanopoulos, except she mispronounces the last name and makes the comparison an active verb. I am often trying to persuade my father in these discussions.

"Don't you see," I say, "the history of the Meos is not so different. In its specificity, yes, but as a part of a tidal wave of powerful conquerors usurping the land of indigenous populations and leading to their systemic erasure and poverty in the present-day, no."

I am thinking of a paragraph I read in one of the many scholarly books that are coming out about Mewat.

"Mewat includes the Aravalli hill ranges, plains and dense forests. Kala Pahad is the black mountain range where the Sultan Firoz Shah Tughlaq constructed a fortress to hunt wild animals. The Aravalli hills once many wild animals such as tigers, panthers, wolves, hyenas, foxes, jackals and deer. In medieval times, Mewat was replete with lakes, seasonal streams, springs and dams. It was lush and green from its descriptions. During Moghul times, the area of Mewat diminishes considerably. Mewat of today is what survives from the 1857 British Mutiny. For eight centuries, Meos resist state authorities. Rebellions against Muslim kings, continuous extermination and frequent famines," the author writes plainly, "are responsible for the decrease in territory."[6]

My father does not disagree. "But what of individual effort?" he insists.

He and I can never agree about structural inequality; he, after all, makes it out. Born into a family of thirteen children where eight of them die, my father is never expected to stay alive. For the first years of his life, his family calls him Hundoo, little one, and does not give him a name for he may die soon too. In the fifty years since he graduates from India's top medical school, AIIMs, few other Meos gain admission there. When we visit India, especially his village, my father is in discomfort. He has seen poverty in such granular closeness that he flinches at distant but still long familiar sights.

"You thrived and see yourself as nothing special," I continue.

"That is not true. I worked hard. Hard work is the only way. I am not saying that there is not corruption," he concedes.

Sometimes, we spend hours talking about relatives. We assess why one is mired in trouble and the other has flourished.

"I do not disagree," I say. "Your hard work and decency is why you are who you are. But still you are a fluke," I continue, "like a falling star or at best, a rare lunar eclipse." *Like Yasin Khan, the Goddess Bedmata inscribed unique lines of destiny on your forehead, too.*

I do not want to dismiss hard work, especially his; I do not know anyone who works as hard as my father.

"Your father does not know how to relax, how to rest," my mother inserts. Even when we are on vacation, my father wakes up early and maps each destination, pushing us to see as much as possible. I did not even know she was paying attention to us.

"Many people word hard," I say, "and still remain in poverty. Why else would you have worked so hard to protect us from being poor?"

The conversation dies down.

I gaze at Crazy Horse from a distance through the glass of the restaurant, uninterested in my own taco salad. I consider the thousands of disappearing indigenous tribes in the world. With histories of dust and sand, no markers for the dead, I cannot help but admire this half-man/half-horse, as he charges in battle and fury.

Crazy Horse

7 Things I Know About Him

1.

He is the first to fawn over a guest to enter his house. He offers local sweets in 7 different varieties just bought from the market. He paces in the courtyard, smokes a cigarette, then inspects the table to see what has not been eaten and asks why. *What else do you want because I will bring it?* And he will. He has that type of heart.

2.

This uncle drinks for much of his life, a preference for whiskey. Why he does not hold a job or take care of his crops. The last of the farmers. For his habit, he is willing to ask anyone for money. The relatives avoid him, everyone except his sister.

3.

He carries a small pocketknife with him. He gifts it once to his niece. It is a moment when he thought he should give her a gift. A small wooden knife that could peel an apple, pick a lock maybe. It is the only thing he has on him of any worth. But it is lovely, that dark chocolate wood.

4.

This uncle gets the disease and no one calls it by its name. His stomach is bloated, he is so angry. He knows he is dying. When his sister visits, he is hopping up and down, blaming her. He knows it is over soon.

5.

When they cut open his stomach for the surgery, it is a mess. As if our insides can be clean or orderly. But even in the world of intestines, there are variations on order and disorder, on the mess of veins, bloods, guts. His insides, the doctors lead everyone to believe, are dirty green, like gutter water.

6.

Before he dies, he spends 7 years applying for an American visa. Some men in Pakistan tell him that he can make money as a cabdriver. Send American dollars back and then everyone will love him. *Wouldn't it be nice to start all over again?*

7.

Where all the people in these spread-out suburbs? He cannot find his special cigarettes. He has to warm food in an electric box. He leaves for Brooklyn and meets the cabdrivers and Dunkin Donuts staff, 4 to a single room, early morning shifts. Long commutes on a bus. This is harder than raising crops. This is for chumps.

He spends one day wandering New York city. He can tell others where the Brooklyn Bridge is and how he fed pigeons in Central Park.

After 7 years of trying to get a visa, he leaves America in 7 days.

Radio Mewat

2012. During my final two years in India, I teach at O.P. Jindal Law School, a premiere global law school, an hour away from Delhi that is yes, in Haryana, my original home state. Colleagues, with graduate degrees from renowned institutions throughout the world, a collection of expats and the Indian elite (from everywhere but Haryana), are tickled by the fact that an American has returned to her home state. One gifts me the Amitav Ghosh novel, *The Hungry Tide,* about an Indian-American woman who returns to South Asia for her research and eventually comes to reside there. Yet, the law school built by a French architect is a contemporary avant-garde modern building that appears to have landed from outer space in the open landscape of the village. Am I still in Haryana? I don't even know.

One afternoon, I speak to a guard who watches over the floor where my office is located.

The guard asks, "Where are you from?"

I tell him the roundabout story and land on Mewat.

"That is a very backward area," he continues. "Girls are not very educated there."

That is true, I say. The literacy rate in Mewat is amongst the lowest in the country.

Another faculty member runs a legal aid clinic in Mewat. I seek him out. He takes me to a legal clinic, only it is not a clinic like I have experienced in the US where individuals assemble, one after another, to be advised about eviction or divorce or foreclosure. Instead, it is a large campground with booths and several hundred Meos sitting in white plastic chairs.

"We are sitting on the dais?" I ask. It reminds me a political function.

A few men are seated. I can see head nods and smiles. It emerges that not only do I bear an American passport but I am also a Meo, rendering me a local and a VIP all at once. My grandfather's daughter and my father's daughter. *An inheritor of family epics,* I want to add, *stymied by the greatness that has come before me.*

After his own speech in eloquent Hindi, the faculty member motions to me from the podium. He asks me to make a speech too.

I am stunned. All my years of Hindi lessons and Urdu lessons and listening to relatives in Mewat is now brought to the test. I hesitantly walk to the podium. The crowd is divided with men sitting on one side and women on the other. If there is ever a moment for an articulate stream of consciousness, then this is the moment.

I begin that yes, I work in this law school and yes, I'm a lawyer and yes, now I'm a faculty member at this global law school in their own backyard. But I am also my father's daughter who as many of you know immigrated to the United States more than thirty years ago (as I say this, I can see my father in flight from his village of Nai Nangla into a wide Meo sky and across two oceans, landing in America as if a stork has brought him there and not an airplane) and the one thing he never feared was educating his daughters because I know some of you fear it (because if you educate your daughter then you will not have control over where she lands up in life) but really, you'll see that this is what is needed, this is what our religion respects, this is what makes my father great. My father educated me and today I am teaching law at a global law school in your state. There is no fear in our faith and our tradition in educating young women.

I sit down.

The faculty member whispers, "See, that went well. Your Hindi is very good."

Afterwards, a few women come up to me, appreciating the message. "What you say is right," one woman, her sari draped over head, says.

A few men gather and pay quick compliments. One stops and stands before me, an evident question on his wrinkled forehead. "Why did you not give the speech in Mewati, your mother tongue?"

Of course.

"I am from Florida!" I exclaim. "People don't speak Mewati there. They don't even speak Hindi really. I learned the language so I can speak to you!"

He looks confused, as if it is somehow impossible that people in Florida do not speak Mewati.

Still, these men are speaking to me in my own right and not as an extension of the men in my family. In fact, none of the men in my family are around. The ones interested in this outreach event unable to make it. It is just me in a sea of Meos.

Afterwards, Radio Mewat, a community radio station, interviews me. The interviewer compliments my Hindi-Urdu. For a non-resident Indian, you speak very well! Now, I see myself in mid-air, landing here in this village on white feathery wings, no longer an expert of ignorance.

My heart is full like an inflated balloon.

VIII.

Inherit

Miras. Inheritance. The word Mirasi comes from Miras which means inheritance. Mirasis are the genealogists or village bards whose oral folktales capture Meo history in ways that history texts do not. As a community of folksingers, Mirasis appear at weddings and the birth of a child in small groups, even in two's. A Mirasi spreads my mother's wedding invitations from one house to another. A Mirasi shares news of Mamu Tayyab's death.

I complain to my mother that neither she, nor anyone else in the family knows the story behind Yasin Khan.

My mother concedes this gap of knowledge with shifty eyes and silence.

The truth is that Mamu Tayyab did know. I did not know enough then to know what or how to ask him. Or I was too afraid. For years, I did not force myself to ask my own questions.

All remaining family members can tell me is that Yasin Khan fought the Raja of Alwar and that he won. The details as bare as a blank page.

2012. When I insist to my mother that she find me Mirasis who do know the history, my cousin's wife arranges for their presence.

One Sunday two Mirasis arrive at the *kothi*. I have them recite all the *dohas* or couplets they know. They recite some by heart; others are written in a red leather-bound book.

My mother, aunts and cousins frown at their book and fragmented couplets; a true Mirasi would have these verses committed to memory and heart.

"Nowadays," they murmur to one another, "Mirasis do not know anything."

Meanwhile my cousin, usually appearing forlorn in light of her domestic troubles, breaks out into a smile and rhyming couplets, reciting them from sheer memory. There is only the skipping music in the room, the delight of the rhyme. It is the well-known couplet about Yasin Khan-

"Raja su Rani Kahe Tu Rehna Ko Jaye
Hun Mile Aasin Tu Wake Paman Pad Jaye

The Queen asks the King to go to Rehna,
Grab hold,
Bow your head near Yasin's feet..."

As the Mirasis recite, I take notes, furiously interpreting their Mewati words into English into my own notebook. I backtrack and ask questions in painstaking detail.

"Were they in the desert or was it the jungle?

"Was this in that year or the following year?"

"Did he really fall from the roof or did someone push him?"

Sometimes, the Mirasis easily answer questions. Other times, they wave their hand and tell me to just listen. "She should really improve her Mewati," they say to my cousin's wife.

For lunch, we feed the Mirasis healthy portions of chicken curry and pullao. The Mirasis share that they go where they are called, exchanging the imprinted history on their tongue for a few rupees but Mewat is changing. In gatherings, their songs have been muted. In fact, the entire place has transformed with the crops diminishing, the land cut up and disputed over. Meos disappearing into the folds of cities with its alleys and makeshift houses and people climbing on top of one another. I see Mirasis disappearing into wealthy homes to dust the dirt off the ground, mutating from village bards to domestic servants. Into factories to weld, carve, stitch.

But what of your songs?

Our songs are not so relevant any more.

The man who passes me on the street in his bicycle and frayed striped shirt might once have been an historian, a teller of tales. He probably still is but only at times. The poetry cut up where time has to be stolen for the words to be pieced together.

After a long afternoon, we give money to each Mirasi for the travel and the poems. They smile, thank us with clasped palms, making their way outside.

A year later when I am on the campus of Jawarhalal Nehru University (JNU) in Delhi, a vestige of Indian leftist politics, Mirasi folksingers are performing in the auditorium. Afterwards, I find them outside, sitting on a mound.

I explain who I am. I am delighted to see a Mirasi performing in Delhi.

Their singer smiles, "We sing about your grandfather!"

"I know," I reply.

Sing me a song about the Aravalli Hills.

He invites me to his hometown in Rajasthan. He even has a business card. He tours abroad. Perhaps all is not lost.

Mirasi performers at JNU

I Retell Mirasi Stories[7]

Story of the Pals

A barefoot juggler, four yellow balls in a single revolution
a snake charmer, billowing head and sizzling tongue
a drummer beating animal skins
a basket weaver crisscrossing pale strands
a grass cutter slitting blades with silver
all five are robbers

The king hears of their bounty
sends his army for their capture

They escape into the wild
onto separate patches of land
cultivating that earth

Soon there are hundreds,
each patch, its own *pal*.
and each *pal*,
Daimrot, Pundlot, Chhiraklot, Nai and Dulot recounts
how they once came

from an escaped
juggler
a snake charmer
a drummer
a basket weaver
and a grasscutter
long, long ago

The Story of Ladh Begum

When the Meo men are ordered
to construct the fortress at Indore
Ladh Begum loses her heart
to the laborer Santhal

She sees him from the palace down below

She sees him placing brick upon brick
to erect the high wall

She flutters her eyelashes
Her father and Santhal helpless
to her want

She and the laborer wed

They find a village together

They give it her name,
Ladhpuri after Ladh Begum

Woman of restless, almond eyes

Hasan Khan ki Katha

In the sixteenth century,
Hasan Khan Mewati
of a neighboring tribe
marries a Meo woman

Now he is Meo too

He sides with the Hindu ruler
Rana Sangha
to fight the Uzbek emperor Babar

He loses his life
in the Battle of Khanwa
leaving only

a crimson sword
for the lions to find
in the Aravalli hills

Dariya Khan Meo and Shashi Badani Mina

A Meo Dariya Khan
marries a Mina Shah Bandani
like a leopard marrying a cheetah

They fight over what to eat

They fall asleep
in the same bed
under the same sun

They lie together
under the fan
of frond-laden trees

Panch Pahar ki Larai

The women break
glass bangles
jump into wells
when the men die,
facing Shahjahan

The emperor will not lower the tax
when the crops do not grow
and the soil is dry, bland

Chaudhry Yasin ki Baat

The princess begs her prince,
Bow your head of turbaned jewels
near the feet of Yasin Khan
Beseech forgiveness
for the suffering you have caused
for the black water
that slips through your feet

The British

> "The Meos have been considered to be remarkable for their lawless and thieving propensities; but in these respects they are now less conspicuous than either Rangurs or Goojurs. I have not seen more beautiful cultivation in India than I have observed in Firozepoor, a purgunah exclusively Meo; and their attachment to the soil a feeling beyond all others strong in India is in this race stronger than in most."
> –William Fraser,
> Agent to the Governor General of India[8]

If one lives in Delhi, one inevitably comes upon the writings of historian and writer William Dalrymple, from personal explorations of the city, to his later finely spun tales that render esoteric Mughal history vivid and poignant stories. His forays into historical Muslim histories first stem from his own personal lineage. I am surprised to find that he too bears some distant connection to the Meos.

William Dalrymple, in his book *City of Djinns,* describes a Scot, William Fraser, a young British Persian scholar who comes to Delhi in 1805 during the colonial period to serve as a Deputy Resident, a posting through the East India Company.[9] As Mughal authority declines, Meo robbers occupy tombs and gardens of Delhi. They render the city and travel beyond the walls unsafe after dark. During his post, Fraser is responsible for subjugating the unruly country of Mewat. In Mewat, Fraser builds a fort. He calls it "Fraser Ghur" where he maintains a thousand sepoys. Meos are classified as a criminal tribe for cattle-lifting and dacoity.

Fraser's immersion in Indian culture encompasses not only his knowledge of Sanskrit texts and Persian couplets. Fraser even befriends and helps the great Urdu poet Ghalib. During that time, Fraser goes "native with a vengeance." He undergoes radical changes in physical appearance. He dons a Rajput moustache and a harem of women. He fathers many children. Dalrymple describes Fraser as Kurtz in *Heart of Darkness* who accepts no challenge to his authority and is deemed insane by his contemporaries, "part severe Highland warrior, part Brahminized philosopher, part Conradian madman."

In Shamsur Rahman Faruqi's masterpiece historical novel, *Mirror of Beauty,* translated from his Urdu novel, *Kai Chaand The Sar-e-Aasmaan,* William Fraser comes to life; so too does his death. An assassin hired by the prince, Nawab Shamsuddin Ahmed Khan ruling over portions of Mewat in a complex series of events kills William Fraser. The British publicly hang the Nawab for Fraser's murder.

In 1857, soldier Mangal Pandey of the 34th Bengal Native Infantry rebels against the East India Company, leading to an anti-British uprising. As natural dissidents and rabble-rousers, Meos are involved in the 1857 rebellion. They pitch battles from village to village in the fight against the British.[10] Meos set police stations, police check posts and custom houses occupied by the British on fire. The British burn down villages. In the central village of Nuh, elephants hoist 52 men up trees to hang them to death.

During the 1857 Mutiny, over 6,000 Meos are killed.

This story of rebellion spills into the twentieth century, involving Yasin Khan and continuing through the Indian Independence Movement of 1947.

The National Archives

2013. After that trip out in the American West, I quit my job and decide to move back to the US to begin a life in writing.

I return to Delhi, unemployed, and sublet an even cheaper barsati in Nizamuddin West with a singular room. My neighbors below are an Afghan refugee family and their children, causing havoc in between raucous giggles. On the days that I am away, the children come to my terrace to play house, rearranging existing furniture of small wooden chairs and tables.

During my remaining time in India, I spend most of my time in a few crucial places. One is the National Archives in New Delhi, its metal shelves lined with colonial papers in mustard folders. The second is the Teen Murti Marg Library which houses old Indian newspapers on microfiche on its second floor.

At the National Archives, my first attempt at historical research, 82 years after the actual peasant uprising, I find Yasin Khan's name in colonial papers. Read. Pause. Record. Scream within. After the Mirasi narration and scholarly readings, I am certain that I can find documents from the colonial era related to my grandfather and the peasant insurgence against the Indian prince, the Raja of Alwar. Yet still, I cannot believe that I actually do find references to him.

It is true, in a big way.

This peasant uprising in 1932 establishes Yasin Khan as the leader of the Meos after the death of Hasan Khan Mewati in 1527. Distinct, his name pops forth from a yellowed page and confirms the stories about him might just exist.

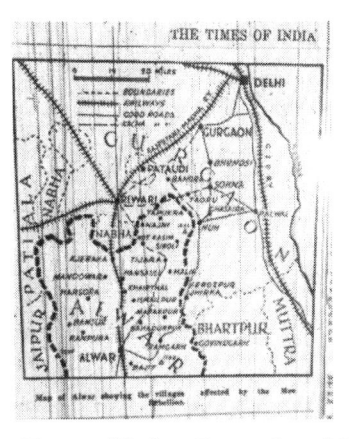

The Times of India, December 1932
Map of Alwar villages affected by the Meo rebellion

Only in these papers, Yasin Khan is accused of being a rabble-rouser, a leader, a divider, a traitor. What he really wants for the Meos was a decrease, a lowering, a fair appropriation of the Raja of Alwar's exorbitant tax. *How does he do what he did?* He aims to close a divide. He aims to quell existing dissent. I want to know how when I do not know much or hardly anything about taxes or guns or the colonial period of 1930s northern India.

How?
How how how
How how how how how how
How how how how how how how

A rogue historian, I spend day after day accumulating references. A few of us are there on a repeated basis; none of us speak to one another, absolved in our work. The staff, buried in offices with heaps of paper, are kind to me. I make photocopies and CDs of everything I can find. So few people spend time in these institutions when there are hundreds of thousands of documents that deserve our scrutiny.

Three months in the archives teach me that the British government preserves many documents but also misplaces, fails to preserve, possibly and probably destroys many documents related to the armed struggle of 90,000 peasants against the Indian Prince of Alwar and which leads to British intervention. Why are the documents articulate in some places and silent elsewhere? The archive stops and starts in unexpected moments.

The documents- official and unofficial correspondences, reports, newspaper articles- that do exist are delicious. Each time I uncover new information, as if I have led myself through a maze and found an exit to my confusion, my heart leaps. I am reminded of Borges' short story, "Aleph" which describes the convergence of a world in a single point found in cellar stairway. That point for me may well be Mewat. The cellar stairway may be dark but the arduous revelation of truths, even partial ones, is full of light.

My name, misspelled, is now in the archives too. In some instances, I am the first person after twenty-three years to flip through these pages. In other cases, other signatures are only thirteen years old and I am in the company of the anthropologists and historians who led me here.

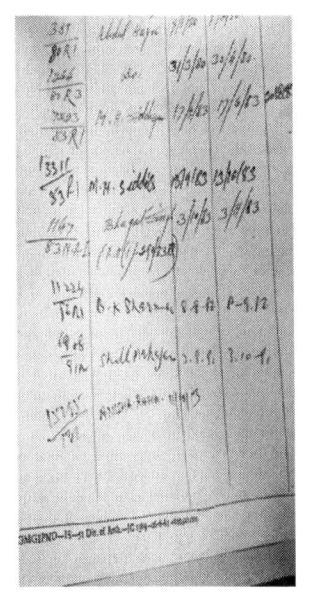

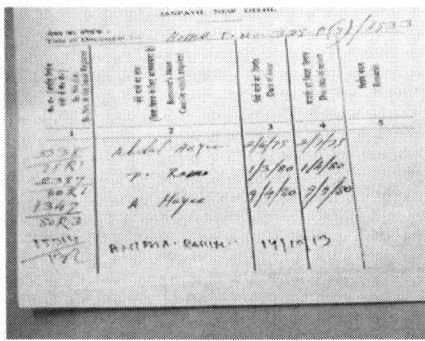

During my breaks, amidst the burning mid-day sun, I not only wander the flowered lawns of The National Archives but also its corridors. In black and white photographs encased in large glass and wooden frames, the Raja of Alwar is always seated in the front row. He appears handsome, regal, arrogant. In one photograph, he sits to the far left with a cane lying casually to the side at a perfect slant. He dons a beret-like hat. His hands are folded in front of his thighs. In another photograph, he sits nearly in the center, the cane between his legs in a perfect pirouette. His black cap contains a gold circular coin in its center. In a third photograph, his legs are crossed, folded hands resting over his thighs. In this photograph, he is least formal, as if he has been wearing authority on his body for years. These fading, yellowing photographs, last vestiges of a different time, suggest that the Raja might have been all the things he was whispered to be.

Raja Jai Singh

Newspaper Articles
related to the 1932-33 Revolt

"Grave Turn to Agitation in Alwar State,"
The Statesmen, November 26, 1932
"Alwar Troops Fire on Meo Rioters"
January 3, 1933
"Alwar Meos on Warpath,"
Times of India, January 3, 1933
"Alwar Village Attacked,"
Times of India, January 4, 1933
"Planes to Fly Over Meo Territory,"
Times of India, January 5, 1933
"Incendiarism and Looting in Alwar State,"
The Statesmen, January 8, 1933
"Disobedience Movement in Alwar State,"
Times of India, January 10, 1933
"British Troops Sent to Alwar State,"
The Statesmen, January 10, 1933
"Collapse of Alwar Rebellion,"
The Times of India, January 11, 1933
"Meos Flee from Alwar State,"
The Statesmen, January 11, 1933
"Restoring Law in Alwar State,"
The Statesmen, January 11, 1933
"Alwar Rebel Area Under Martial Law,"
Times of India, January 12, 1933
"Troops Visit Disturbed Alwar Areas,"
The Statesmen, January 12, 1933
"More Troops for Alwar,"
The Times of India, January 13, 1933
"How Alwar Was Saved from Meo Conflagration,"
Times of India, January 13, 1933
"Meos' Friendly Welcome to British Troops,"
Times of India, January 14, 1933
"All Quiet in Alwar,"

Hindustan Times, January 14, 1933
"Troops Busy in Alwar State,"
The Statesmen, January 14, 1933
"Troops Fire on Alwar Rebels,"
The Times of India, January 16, 1933
"Alwar Disturbance Finally Quelled,"
Times of India, January 23, 1933
"Meos Still Not Satisfied,"
The Hindustan Times, March 22, 1933

The Biography of Yasin Khan: A Text and its Rendering

2013. I run my hands over the pages of a biography of Yasin Khan. Two years ago, my cousin gifts me Hakim Ajmal Khan's biography from his cupboard in the village of Nuh. *Bhaiyya ki kitab.* It is priced at two hundred rupees, roughly four US dollars.

The biography is written in Urdu. I put out an ad for a translator but do not receive favorable responses and instead hire an Urdu tutor; I will read the book myself. For months, three days in a week, in between my time at the National Archives and the Teen Murti Marg Library, the Urdu tutor in a South Delhi enclave walks me through the biography, page by page. Page after page.

The tutor, a pleasant man with glasses, asks me over and over, during our lessons, "Is this really where you came from?" *Is this really who you are?* "You must share this," he repeats.

The burden and the responsibility and the exhilaration of being the storyteller of history's ghosts. I feel the weight of the biography in contrast to the colonial record. How a different vantage point yields an entirely new story.

"I will," I assure him.

Here is what we learn.

~

When Hakim Ajmal Khan first sees Yasin Khan, the latter is dressed in a sherwani, a long coat, trousers and a Turkish hat of oblong velvet with a black tassel. They meet again in June 1945 at the All-India Meo Conference. A poem is read at the gathering, *Meri pyari Mewat, mera vatan haim.* My beautiful Mewat, my country.

The Partition of India and Pakistan is the largest human migration to date.

When I ask my mother and father about Partition, they are too young to remember. No relative mentions or speaks of Partition on their own. My aunt shares a few details, then switches to another topic.

I learn about Partition through texts.

In 1947 during the Partition of India and Pakistan, a mob descends onto a Meo village. The village must be evacuated. Hakim Ajmal Khan's father, Abdul Shakur, is writing an account of the history of the Meos. Before fleeing, Hakim Ajmal Khan, deposits his father's text in the grain store. The family runs into the forest to escape the mob. When they return, his father's first question is *where is the text*. The house and the library are burnt down but the text remains whole.

Meos make plan to migrate to Pakistan.

Yasin Khan insists they remain in India. Tales abound that Yasin Khan lies down on Sohna Road to stop the movement.

The police come after him; a woman conceals him with a razai-blanket.

Yasin Khan arranges, in secret, for Gandhi to visit the village of Ghasera. When Gandhi speaks, he says that the Meos are the *rirrh,* the backbone of this nation. A third of Meos migrate to Pakistan; two-thirds remain in India.

Yasin Khan spends three months in jail. When he leaves jail, he has a long beard of ringlets, black checkered marks on his cheeks, a head of crawling lice.

Yasin Khan does not save many documents. He keeps his records at the *kothi* after its construction is finished.

During Partition, the rioters search the *kothi* and burn his papers.

After 1947, Yasin Khan is occupied with the movement of refugees. His comings and goings in the villages increase. He rushes from place to place to raise spirits.

Hakim Ajmal Khan and Yasin Khan meet the year following Partition. His father is also absorbed with the Central Relief Council and sends Hakim Ajmal Khan to compile a list of displaced persons, make a roster, tabulate the numbers. At his father's urging, whenever there is a program or a function, Hakim Ajmal Khan attends and avails himself of Yasin Khan's hospitality.

~

Some years later, at a village council, Mamu Tayyab insists that there must be a biography of Yasin Khan; Hakim Ajmal Khan must be the one to write it. Hakim Ajmal Khan already has this intention but when the gathering speaks his name, it spurs him, and his motivation grows, bursting open like a flower. He accepts this responsibility, *kabul kar diya,* right then and right there, placing this trust in him in a pocket over his heart.

Hakim Ajmal Khan relies on Mamu Tayyab's memory of Yasin Khan's life after Partition. He depends on clippings from the *Meo Gazette.* He seeks friends with records and some documents. "All we have," Hakim Ajmal Khan writes, "are the memories that Yasin Khan carried, that others carried of him." *All that we have are the memories that Yasin Khan carried, that others carried of him.*

All those who witness the Alwar Movement, the uprising against the Raja in 1932, die one after another, *Allah ke pyare.* Chaudhry Abdul Haye, another freedom fighter, accumulates documents in the National Archives about the Alwar Movement. I find his name in the archives. He never does complete or publish his writings. He dies in his home near the Jama Masjid where refugees occupy its steps and the Alwar Movement reaches its height.

I wonder too where his words remain.

The *kothi* has not finished construction and is only completed in 1953. Meanwhile, Yasin Khan stays in the mosque facing the *kothi.* Hakim Ajmal Khan meets him there. He travels difficult roads and narrow alleys to reach him.

From 1959 to 1961, Hakim Ajmal Khan stays with Yasin Khan all the time. He insists that Yasin Khan note the incidents of his life. Yasin Khan avoids his demands, "Do good and throw it in the well!" *Neki kar aur kuan main daal.*

~

Hakim Ajmal Khan searches in libraries for copies of the epic Meo *Mahabharata*. It is rumored that its only existing copy is dropped in a well. What all would we find in the wells of Mewat?

A Meo *Mahabharata*, my grandfather's good deeds floating in its water.

~

1957. Ten years after the Partition of India and Pakistan, Yasin Khan begins to fall ill. He lies in his charpoy for hours at a time. Abdul Shakur keeps him in his home for twenty-two days. He has him treated. Hakim Ajmal Khan too takes care of him. Yasin Khan does not take his medicine on time. Nor does he rest properly. No one can force him either. The doctors do not give him allopathic medicine. Rather, they administer electric shock. They do not have a name for his sickness. It is labeled a disease of the mind.

Saadat Hassan Manto's story, "Toba Tek Singh" about the exchange of inmates in an asylum between India and Pakistan comes to mind as the seminal story of Partition. Only those who are ill, speak the truth of the rupture of the Indian subcontinent. Its inherent madness.

To keep Yasin Khan busy on the days he feels restless and confused, the doctor tells him to play chess. Yasin Khan searches for opponents. Whomever does not look busy is beckoned.

Many times, Hakim Ajmal Khan plays; Yasin Khan beats him every time.

For twenty-four years after Partition, Yasin Khan works daily even when he is sick. He spends his days in one place. He spends his nights in another. He goes from Raisena, Santa Vardi, Nuh, Rehna, to Delhi, Gurgaon, Jama Masjid, Chandigarh.

~

Hakim Ajmal Khan experiences neck and other bodily pains which delay the completion of the biography. In 2008, it is published in a hardback brown cover.

Decades later, after its initial drafts, I find this text.

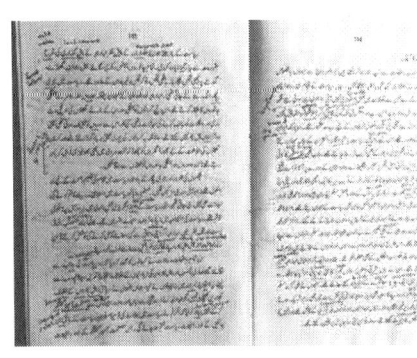

A Timeline of Activities

(according to the biography by Hakim Ajmal Khan)

1919- Yasin Khan begins meeting with people because of the cooperative societies work. People seek advice from him. He is not a victim of changing political parties. He becomes a Cooperative Inspector.

1926 to 1946- Yasin Khan becomes a member of the Council Assembly and the Punjab Legislative Assembly. He is responsible for constructing roads in Mewat and a primary school in every village. He creates canals. He builds rest houses. He establishes a hospital and an animal hospital.

1932-1933- A peasant movement arises against the high taxes and corruption of the Raja of Alwar. Yasin Khan emerges as a leader of the movement. The Yasin Brayne Meo High School is the political nucleus of the uprising. Because of the defeat of the Raja of Alwar, Yasin Khan is designated the leader of the Meo community, *Chaudhriyon ka Chaudhry*. He is the first such designated leader since Hasan Khan Mewati in 1527.

1933 to 1945- there are 409 cases filed against Yasin Khan. A plea is made that it's not of benefit to the institution to have all these pending cases. Charges of embezzlement are found to be false. Conservative clerics do not tire of warning Meos about the evil influence of English education, deeming the Yasin Brayne Meo High School a Satanic institution. Yasin Khan develops enemies for his rise in the community. The District Commissioner of Police (DCP) wants Yasin Khan to apologize but he refuses. The DCP attempts to take away his lawyering license in the Punjab High Court. Yasin Khan fights his own case; he is successful.

1947- Partition. Yasin Khan is opposed to Meos leaving Mewat and settling in Pakistan. He fears they will lose all their land rights. He arranges for Gandhi to speak at the village of Ghasera. Refugees seek shelter in the Yasin Brayne Meo High School.

1952- Yasin Khan becomes an MLA in the Punjab Assembly. At the time, the Unionist Party, a farmer's party, is in power. Yasin Khan works closely with Chotu Ram, a peasant from the neighboring Hindu Jat community of the Unionist Party.

1962- Chaudhry Kamal Khan, a member of Yasin Khan's own *pal*, now in Pakistan comes to meet Yasin Khan. The Indian government deems Chaudhry Kamal Khan a spy. Chaudhry Kamal Khan is arrested, put in an ice-bed as a form of torture, then taken to Amritsar. Yasin Khan demands to know his whereabouts; he speeds to him. He rescues Kamal Khan, one foot in jail, then seats him in the car and deposits him at the Wagah border of India and Pakistan. Yasin Khan resigns from being Deputy Minister of Punjab.

Repeatedly, Yasin Khan is deemed a rebel.

Hakim Ajmal Khan writes that Yasin Khan is unconcerned with awards. The work, always, interests him most.

To the biographer Hakim Ajmal Khan, Yasin Khan is the poet Iqbal's "ideal man."

He is the ideal man until his mind breaks down, exhausted by the weight of the churnings for freedom and justice. He too grows tired.

To me, he is a mystery. The reason I wander graveyards, in the open or in the bookstacks, tracing his footsteps.

Widowed

Eighteen days after Sabina is born, Yasin Khan arrives at my father's home, my mother's *susraal*, and kisses a tender baby girl on the forehead, giving her a name that means daughter of the moon. The women in the house rush to bring him water, only he refuses. He has heard the complaints that the first birth is that of a girl. "I will not even take a glass of water from a home," he says, "where there is sadness over the birth of a girl." He storms out.

My mother who is rushing to make him tea, dropping small slabs of wood into the fire, throws a *dupatta* over her head, treading on soft dirt after him. "Bhaiyya, stop, stop! Have a cup of tea at least…"

He keeps walking.

On February 19, 1971, twenty-seven days after he last sees my mother and Sabina, after he visits with the beggar Nishad downstairs, after he blows a whisper on his grandson's forehead to make the fever subside, after he pats his wife's soft greying hair one very last time, after he visits the village of Ghasera where Gandhi once set foot, after he makes the comment *I won't sleep in this house made of interest* and says *I am the whole world's father, whatever you want to give me, give me now,* Chaudhry Yasin Khan dozes off to sleep and does not awake.

A heart attack in the night.

For days, he speaks of four strange men following him. Late one morning, he does not come out of his room. The servants rattle the door, then cut the lock. He will never awake again.

"Chaudhrani," the villagers crouching near her bed, my grandmother swathed in a white blanket, staring feebly at those gathered, say, "you are not the only who is widowed. All of Mewat is a widow today."

In the village of Nuh, hundreds of thousands gather, grabbing handfuls of dirt to shower onto his grave outside of the college he helps to build. They beat their chests as his body is lowered into the ground. Those who cannot control themselves are told to have *sabr*, patience. The people grow hollow as the grave is no longer visible, making a home deep in the center of the earth.

The milk in my mother's breasts dries up.

My grandmother can no longer sleep and lies on his grave at night, waking with the first rays of light. Her home no longer a home.

Forty days after his death, there is the *jhelum* ceremony and the family is gifted an elephant which my mother traverses on as an ordinary traveler.

For months, there are rumors of an apparition that saunters on the school grounds. A milky silhouette that cannot be ignored, only too faint to be properly seen.

IX.

My Mother Speaks

I would like to say that my mother and I sit down one afternoon and she tells me everything she knows that I want to know. But it is not like that.

Rather, over many years, she reveals snippets and always in unexpected moments. Her mind wanders but when she loses herself in reverie, then I cannot stop listening.

Now I do not know where her voice ends and mine begins.

"I have the best stories."

You do, I say.

"You children laugh when I tell you these stories. You say I am like that foolish character on television who remembers home in a laughable place. Yes, Rose from *Golden Girls*."

It is true, we do.

"Backward, to be forgotten."

For our highways free of bovine and our relationships full of doors.

"But what do you kids know with your television and phones and racing hearts?"

Where the people we listen to the most speak to us from a box that can go numb and fragile like static?

"*Bewakoof!* Fools. I have stories, the very best stories."

You do, I say. Now tell me a few!

"I called your grandfather Bhaiyya which means 'brother' because I only heard bhaiyya-bhaiyya from the beginning."

The Goddess Bedmata inscribed unique lines of destiny on his forehead. The Mirasis say the lines came in a collection of three. You peered closely at Bhaiyya, drawing yourself up to him on bended knees in search of those lines, but did not find them. When he looked at you curiously, you scurried away.

"Bhaiyya's father, Chaudhry Khuda Baksh Khan, drowned soon after Bhaiyya was born. Chasing his buffalo into the pond, Khuda Baksh walked into the water and never came out. From then on, Bhaiyya's uncle, Wali-ji, raised Bhaiyya."

There are slivers of power in a Wali-ji like an electric current that dislodges you just so. Slivers passed on.

"'He is a boy,' his mother said. 'What if I die and there is no one?' Bhaiyya marries four times. Even I do not know the whole story but the first marriage occurred when he was seven years of age."

There are laws against these things.

"Nowadays, one hardly understands. Like how the Hindu woman some houses away was married to a tree. Now there are laws against marrying a child or a tree which even if people still do not follow makes the public gasp a bit. I know, I've heard the sucking in of air. But then, things happened and the gasping public felt far away from us. But his five-year-old wife, whom he only met twice, once during a game of hopscotch, then on the wedding day, died of smallpox. Then Bhaiyya married a woman from the village of Roopra. Together they had my half-brother, Mohammad Hussain. He lived in Pakistan after Partition so I did not know him very well. Roopra too died when malaria descended."

Like a big, black tent that has been erected over a house.

"After death snatched the bride from Roopra, Bhaiyya married a woman from the village of Felandy."

But even though she tried it all- prayers at a grave, a tabiz around her neck to ward off evil spirits- not a single seed sprouted.

"One afternoon, her three brothers in a concerned line said, 'Marry again, Yasin Sahib, a great man like you should bear children.' Mai. My mother."

Moon-faced Jhummi from Tikhri, the most *maluk* of them.

"She gave birth to seven of us. What fun we all had growing up together. Akhtari was the most beautiful. Asghari, the most tender. Surwuri, the sharpest tongue."

And you, cradled in love.

"Tayyab was like Bhaiyya. Hamid was the most beautiful. And Asghar, coddled. Together life was a *mela*, an ongoing festival."

You could only assume that it would remain like that forever.

"Of the seven, I am the youngest girl and second to youngest of the siblings. Loved, terribly by Bhaiyya, by Mai. My birth date is unknown but I was born around 1947 in the village of Rehna, a midwife nursing Mai through labor pangs."

"Bhaiyya loved Mai. Mai used to sit in a circle of women goos-pussing, 'Do not disturb your mother,' Bhaiyya would say. 'She is holding a meeting.'"

His eyes sparkling a bit.

"I too sit close to Mai during those gatherings, place her feet in my palms and massage the soles just so."

The way I am right now? I ask. It is true; I massage my mother's feet. I know her feet like they are my hands.

"Kneading it, like it is bread. Hours can by like this with my hands working up and down her shins, rubbing the soles, listening to stories... But wait, I am supposed to be telling you about Bhaiyya. To return to what I remember."

Yet memory is like water which slips through crevices and dissolves into the earth. Enough for today.

"This is all I want to remember now."

"Yes, yes, let's begin again. So persistent! There is a fly in your head and it whirrs and doesn't stop, does it?"

If it were not for this fly, no one would learn this history.

"Bhaiyya is Mewat's first lawyer, studying in Aligarh and Delhi. He makes sure his daughters do not remain unlettered like the rest."

What did he do as a lawyer?

"He argued criminal cases. On the days that his cases were listed, Bhaiyya rose before the sun cracked open and read extra nafl prayers."

As if remaining in *sajda* on folded thighs and knees would bring him nearer to the earth, to the sound of his own thumping heart.

"Mai too makes a prayer-dua. Surwuri and I make sure his clothes are pressed, his breakfast ready. 'Arre oh, Chameli, where have you gone and died? Press this coat for Bhaiyya- *abhi!*' Chameli, the house servant, who slept upstairs would come running."

A look of partial apology as she scoops his clothes in a bundle.

"Sometimes, we walk him down all four flights of the *kothi*; those are the days before the lift is installed. We stay on the top floor and rent out the remaining three. On the ground floor, they salaam Bhaiyya."

The hungry, in tattered, greying clothes, huddled or outstretched.

"These poor souls whom Bhaiyya distributed blankets in winter and plates of pullao on Eid might be the same ones he saw in Court, pleading before the judge. 'Chau Sahib, help us,' they say, hands folded together."

Not like now, I sigh, where there is fear of the poor, disdain for their cries of money and assistance.

"The poor too have multiplied and now they are everywhere and the streets beyond the *kothi* are so flooded with the public... Mai would complain that Bhaiyya gave away everything to the poor. But still, she let him."

Loose change dripping out of pockets. Worn rupees finding their way into dirt-ridden palms.

"Meos honored Bhaiyya as Chaudhriyon ka Chaudhry, the Leader of all our leaders. Once, small hands groped in the crowd to speak to Bhaiyya, 'Let her through,' he said. An aged woman asked, 'Chaudhry Sahib, where were you when beauty was being doled out?' Bhaiyya was ruddy skinned. Not *khubsoorat*–beautiful like Mai. 'In the house of intellect!' he responded."

Everyone laughed.

"Bhaiyya could never belong only to us. To his blood. This, we knew. My brother Tayyab most of all, slipping into his footsteps even before Bhaiyya left us. Bhaiyya pulled here and there."

Maybe he too knew this when he was pouring through books near candlelight. When Wali-ji took him on upward trudges in the Black, Black Hills.

"Bhaiyya and a sympathetic Britisher build a school in the heart of Nuh. In the school, Bhaiyya sees a young boy from the village of Nai Nangla. When Abdur Rahim is the first in his family to gain college admission and leave Mewat, Bhaiyya arrives at his single room in Gurgaon one afternoon, seats himself on the room's lone wooden chair and discusses the need for a college dormitory for Meos to study outside of the village. Abdur Rahim does not have a kitchen but there is one down the hall. He asks the maid to quickly make a cup of tea. But before the leaves had boiled, Bhaiyya takes leave. He decides then that I would marry Abdur Rahim. A confidant says to him that Chaudhry sahib, this boy comes from such a small village. He is not a match for your daughter."

And what does he say?!

"'You do not know.' Bhaiyya says, looking at a map just then, 'This boy will travel the world.'"

"At the wedding procession, Abdur Rahim wore a proud turban and jostled in on an elephant, decorated with a red and gold sequined saddle. My friends gathered on the rooftop and watched him pass with the *baraat*. Running into my bedroom, one *lalee* giving a thud to another on the shoulder, falling over and bending in laughter. They exclaimed, 'He is so earnest. I just wanted to snatch him off the elephant!' For three days, our house of four levels was filled. Streets paved with thousands of people. Endless food."

Chaudhry Yasin's youngest daughter was now married.

"When I left, I did not understand that I was leaving. Or I did understand. Because I could not eat on the plane ride over. He forced me to have a bite in Paris. Some bread, some chicken. I said no, this food tastes like nothing. I did not leave the house at first. This small apartment."

Musty, green-colored.

"I folded Sabina's hand into mine."

"We raised you children in this faraway place. My mood lightened somehow. I began to wear saris. I could be seen laughing in a purple one with a gold necklace dangling around my neck. But when I returned, I wept in my mother's arms. My bhabhi, my brother's arms."

Your weeping, a song.

"All of us seven children married, each bearing two boys and two girls. I did not want to marry. I wanted to stay with Mai forever- jannat-heaven is in a mother's feet- and she might have kept me next to her."

The soles of her feet in your palms.

"I still remember the day that she died. I learned of it over the telephone, alone at home. Abdur Rahim was at work, the black plastic receiver against my ear."

"'*Lalee,* I do not understand what you are saying. Say it, say it again.' I thought I had misunderstood Surwuri."

The world had cracked in two.

"Tears pounded against the heart, up the throat, through my eyes. The dull ache of the head as the water fills up and you think you might drown...Only I couldn't. I had to pick you children up from the bus stop. How the tears would not stop rolling onto the Nova's midnight blue steering wheel..."

"My youngest, Anisa, is moody."

Why are you telling me about me?

"I know this is about you. But this should be in your book too!"

"She reads all days, holed up in her books."

Her moods like phases of the moon. A quarter, a half moon, a full moon. You feel it.

"Her storm rising."

As the glow in the sky becomes more yellow, more perfect.

"I try to teach her how to cook. She gets angry when I do not let her fry the *puris*. 'How will I ever learn?' she says. She does not even listen."

She listens.

"She trods off into her pink room upstairs. I yell from

the kitchen. Yell to her father seated in the living room watching *60 Minutes* about this *Nakammi-forsaken-Allaud*. She comes back down with a pout but stands next to me near the stove silently. I show her again."

She is always listening.

"This time, she listens."

Mom's Dessert Recipes

Zharda

4-6 Servings

Boil five to six cups of water.

Wash two cups of rice and add in boiling water.

Cook the rice. I add yellow food coloring.

Drain the water and pour the rice once it is cooked.

On medium heat, put three spoons of oil (you can use vegetable oil or *ghee*).

Put green cardamom and seeds of black cardamom or *moti elaichi* which you need to peel beforehand.

Once the seeds grow larger in the oil, then put in sugar and 3/4ths cup of water.

Stir and let the sugar dissolve. It will become a thin paste.

Then add rice to the mixture.

Cover it half-way. Let it cook till all the water evaporates.

Put it in low heat as the water disappears.

Garnish with raisins, chopped almonds and pistachios.

Shakrana

4-6 Servings

Boil five to six cups of water.

Wash two cups of rice and add in boiling water.

Cook the rice. Drain the water and keep the rice once it is cooked in a *chalni* (drainer bowl). Pour the rice in plates.

Add sugar. In Mewat, we use *boorah*, a special type of sugar. Warm *ghee* (clarified butter) and pour it over the rice in each plate.

Serve hot. Eat immediately.

X.

The Train

1.

My mother's sister dies last week. My mother says, she was not old or sick. But I knew that she was. I had seen her brittle bones, fading memory, displaced thoughts. She thought I was my mother.

Still, I know it is like this. Each person fades, to be laid below the earth.

And when my mother cries, it is as if her heart is being ripped.

Last year there were three deaths. Her older brother, followed by his wife two months later, and in between the younger brother. *The village is dying.*

I make a hospital visit to see my uncle on a bed, a hydrangea of plastic tubes.

For once, I am in the right place at the right time because he dies soon after we leave the hospital. I mourn his death as if he is my brother with a house full of Meo women, reciting prayers on beads, beads falling into bowls as if he is being lowered into the earth with the utterance of each word. *The village is dying.* I do not bother with the two funerals that follow. Instead, I fall in love. I am tired of death and decide that life must triumph.

With each death, a piece of my mother is being taken out. And when she sobs, it is the horrible cry of a child, as if memory is being shattered, a wrongful taking away.

2.

In that same week our neighbor's mother dies. They hold a gathering in the temple that they call a celebration to speak of this woman who lives eighty-plus years. Everyone recalls her laugh, her penchant for reading, her fondness for gatherings, the tennis sneakers she wears underneath her sari as she takes an evening walk.

A woman sings for her. And her own daughter relays a dream from the night before, her mother wearing her favorite blazing red sari and boarding a train. *I worried she would not find the right compartment.*

But I'll find it, she tells her. And the train departs.

That night I tell my mother you too must celebrate. Death is not just death.

If others leave, it is not your loss alone. They too have to be elsewhere.

Beads

Google Alert

2014. Before moving back to the US, I reassure my relatives; it is for good this time.

Just before I leave, a brutal gang rape occurs that sparks international alarm. For years, I travel and live in Delhi with a hyper-awareness of what it means to be a woman. I know what it is to be groped on public buses and large crowds, stared and cat-called at on city streets, and flashed by a man who pulls up next to me in his car asking for directions to Lodi Garden. When the gang rape occurs and women pour into the streets of the Capital in protest with candles, India Gate awash with small lights, the churnings of change for a life less difficult and brutal make themselves felt.

Delhi too suffers pollution at levels that diminish life expectancy by five years, a permanent smog lacing its sky. One by one, expat friends move to other parts of the world.

I travel from one village after another to bid adieu to family. I sit on charpoys, sip tea, let relatives run their hands over my head. Do not forget India, they insist. They hand me a wad of rupees before I get inside the jeep.

On this final departure, I linger at the last village. A cousin remarks, "Even when you were little, you insisted on climbing up the Aravalli mountains."

"That cannot be true," I say. I am sure he must be mistaken. Even if I had given up the lull and familiarity of the ocean to trek in the lush green of maple and oak trees in the Himalayan mountains, I am unable to stand anywhere near the edge. I hold onto the person next to me with dear life.

"People must fall all the time!" I once declare. The guide reassures me, the only living being that has fallen below was a sheep. The people find him later floating down the river in the valley. Only those are mountain people, I insist, whose children run up and down the trails with agility, ease and a vibrancy that infuses their faces. Still, I make it to the top where there are only sheep, rippling white fur bodies all around. Nothing else matters at the very top of the mountain...

I return to my cousin.

"No, you did." He smiles, "You were always wanting to climb the mountain."

At the end of this journey, I am left with a treasure trove of images, documents, stories, and records. One evening, on a December night when the nights have grown cold enough for a sweater and a shawl and faint stars are visible amongst the Delhi smog, Balaji Couriers comes to my barsati to ship my boxes.

When I return to the US, at first, there is the unbearable resounding silent void of people and places that can no longer be seen or touched or heard. I wake up some mornings filled with tears; I snap with unexpected anger in the middle of the day. Sometimes, the void is a ringing sound in my ears. Will the silence ever be filled? When a tribe splits, splinters, everyone in the tribe suffers the effects. Out of place, after years of a life lived elsewhere, I am given advice to think of home not as a geographical place but in my writing itself.

No longer cutting up time and geography, I set my email to receive Google Alerts about Mewat. Why must everything be about its lack, its scarcity, its decline? In just a month, all of the articles are about Meo gangs, or children dying of malaria, or the lack of government doctors in rural clinics, or a scam involving stolen funds for children's schoolbooks and rations. Is there an American parallel? A fellow-writer in my writing workshop pens a red-ink comment at the end of my story about Partition: "Meos are the real Indians."

Narendra Modi too rises to power. During his tenure, violence against minorities, particularly Muslims intensifies. News reports about a 2016 gang rape of Meo women relate to the consumption of beef. How the police raid villages to search for beef in biryani. The city of Gurgaon is renamed Gurugram to sanskritize its name. Cow vigilantes on the Jaipur National Highway assault a Meo farmer, Pehlu Khan who dies soon after but his post-mortem claims his death is not related to the assault. Lack of prosecution sparks outrage over 'no one killed Pehlu Khan', leading to Muslim Lives Matter/Not in My Name protests. Cow vigilantes assault another Meo young man on the train. Mewat is everywhere in the news. On *NPR*, the *New York Times*, *The Guardian*.

After Pehlu Khan dies, the Mirasis compose these couplets[11]–

Bapu Ghasera Aayo
Hindu Muslim Sab Samjhayo
Angrezon Ne Phoont Ger Di
Aaj Unke Moond Laga Deo Talo

Bapuji came to Ghasera
Got Hindus and Muslims to embrace each other
The British drove a wedge between us
But were left tongue-tied forever

Pehla dukh Dingerheri
Duja Pehlu Maar Diya
Junaid Khan Chalti Gaadi Mein
Kuch Gundon Ne Maar Diya
Ghar se College Gaya tha Padhne
Aaj Talak Nahin Aaya
Maa Ki Akhiyan Taras Gayi
Najeeb Laal Nahi Aya

First, the horror in Dingerheri
Second, the killing of Pehlu
Junaid Khan while on a moving train
Was lynched by a raging mob

He went to college
And what transpired is unknown
His mother's still waiting
but Najeeb never came home

Kaise Kaise Zulm Ho Chuke
Bigda Bhaichara
Bharat Tha Sone Ki Chidiya
Narak Bana Diya Sara

Various atrocities took shape soon after
Our brotherhood witnessed a never before rupture
What was once a golden bird
The India of yore – now a living hell

Hindu Muslim Sikh Isai
Bigda Bhaichara
Bharat Tha Sone Ki Chidiya
Narak Bana Diya Sara

Hindus, Muslims, Sikhs, Christians
In peace did dwell
What was once a golden bird
The India of yore – now a living hell

I attend US academic conferences, speaking about Mewat, its history, my family's history and the current political violence. I read portions of this memoir, nervous beforehand, sweaty palms and an aching stomach, as if the words and this journey must not be entirely real. But as I shatter preconceptions, words blowing translucent bubbles across conference rooms and microphones, I am in the right place, at the right time.

Good Books

My mother tells everyone that I am writing a book. I am no longer going "backwards" but retrieving, preserving. Friends and relatives ask me about the book intermittently. The book is no longer a fanciful or wild, buried dream. My father too reads a draft. I publish my first photo-essay about Mewat in a high school publication decades ago. His friends admire my photographs, finding beauty in those images; he is embarrassed and asks why I wanted to write about such a place. I hesitate now when he reads these pages in a single sitting in the armchair. When he finishes, he concedes, "You did the research on Yasin Khan that I was never able to. I went to the National Archives but…"

"My social sciences background should count for something. You do not mind that I am writing about Mewat?"

I am hoping this book will get published but none of my family will read it.

"It is your book and you should write what you want," he says.

I am silent for once, mouth hanging open. *Is this a dream?*

In high school, I sneak away to my room to write, fighting off demands for household work to vacuum the living room or chop onions. Now, when perched at a white desk in a room lined with pink and white flowered wallpaper, I tell my mother to let me finish this sentence or thought. Instead of further interrupting, she says, "Go, go, do your work."

During the following summer, after my first year at an MFA program in creative writing, I venture to East Harlem for a talk on memoir and family history at La Casa Azul Bookstore.

A cab driver on 116th and Lexington asks me, "Where are you from?"

"Why does it matter?" I ask.

"You could be from anywhere," he says.

I laugh. I often feel like I am from everywhere and nowhere and somewhere very, very small all at once.

I ask him again, "Where is Lexington Avenue?"

"You are headed to the bookstore. It's the next block.'

"How did you know that is where I was headed?"

"Because they sell good books there and you look like you read good books."

And it is as if he knows that now it is here, in these pages, writing and reading and remembering and reconstructing, where I might just reside.

***

Endnotes

1 Arthur Rimbaud, "Drunken Boat."

2 Willie Perdomo, VONA poetry workshop 2014.

3 Chowdhry Abdul Haye in his essay, "The Freedom Movement in Mewat and Dr. K.M. Ashraf" in *Kunwar Mohammad Ashraf* (People's Publishing House, 1969), pgs. 291-336.

4 Suraj Bhan Bhardwaj's, *Contestations and Accommodations: Mewat and Meos in Mughal India*, pg. 15.

5 Derived from Bhardwaj, pg.55.

6 Bhardwaj, pg.12.

7 Derived from Bhardwaj summaries of folk tales.

8 A. Fraser, *Statistical Report of Zillah Gurgaon* (Lahore: n. 1846), pg. 15 cited in Bhardwaj.

9 William Dalrymple, *City of Djinns,* (Penguin Books, 2003) pgs. 98-114.

10 Zakir Hussain, "Delhi, Meos and the Great Uprising: A Study of Anti-British Resistance during 1857," Indian History Congress, 20th Session, Department of History, University of Delhi, May 15-17, 2010.

11 https://www.thequint.com/videos/short-doqs/meo-muslims-of-mewat-sing-of-india-of-lynchings-dadri-akhlaq-and-najeeb

Author's Acknowledgements

Many people helped this book come into existence.

Thank you, in chronological order,

constant friends, Catarina Pedreiro, Amy Paul and Nick Robinson in this writing journey

beloved high school English instructor, JBO (John Boyd Ogden, 1932-2020).

Leandre Jackson, passionate mentor for these photographic images

2014 VONA Poetry Workshop at UC Berkeley with Willie Perdomo

The tremendous Rutgers Newark faculty of 2014-2016 with instructors Jayne Anne Philipps, Rigoberto Gonzalez, Brenda Shaughnessy, Akhil Sharma and Tayari Jones

Alice Elliot Dark for instilling urgency and courage and craft

2015 Ithaca Image Text workshop led by Catherine Taylor and Nicholas Muellner

fellow Rutgers classmates, those workshops were everything, especially writer-friends Safia Jama and Laura Spence Ash

John Keene, brilliant and kind thesis advisor, opening a path of hybridity and non-linear storytelling with sustaining encouragement

2017 University of Hawaii-Manoa on Pedagogy and Community Building organized by Sai Bhatawadekar where I read aloud initial pages

Center for Fiction, A Public Space and Elizabeth Gaffney whose full-length manuscript workshops led me to the finish line

fellowship APS workshop readers, particularly Eunice Kim, for critical open-hearted feedback

Jersey City Writers, Sarah Jewell, Nirupa Umapathy, and Poetry Plum workshops for community

Mary Ann Koruth, Tim Raphael and the team at *Newest Americans* for publishing initial pages and giving it first breathe

mentor De Miller (1944-2021), who believed in this book before it was written

my family around the globe, in our colorfulness, are the heart and muse

my mother, Afsari Begum Rahim (1947-2021), who did not live to see its completion but resides in these pages

ANISA RAHIM is a writer, photographer and public interest lawyer. Her writing has been published widely including the anthology *New Moons: Contemporary Writing by North American Muslims*, edited by Kazim Ali (Red Hen Press). She received an MFA in Creative Writing from Rutgers-Newark. See more of her work at anisarahim.com.